Collins

TREASURE HOUSE

Teacher's Guide 5
Composition Skills

Authors: Sarah Snashall and Chris Whitney

HarperCollins Publishers
Since 1817

William Collins' dream of knowledge for all began with the publication of his first book in 1819.

A self-educated mill worker, he not only enriched millions of lives, but also founded a flourishing publishing house. Today, staying true to this spirit, Collins books are packed with inspiration, innovation and practical expertise. They place you at the centre of a world of possibility and give you exactly what you need to explore it.

Collins. Freedom to teach.

Published by Collins
An imprint of HarperCollins*Publishers*
The News Building
1 London Bridge Street
London
SE1 9GF

Browse the complete Collins catalogue at
www.collins.co.uk

© HarperCollins*Publishers* Limited 2017

10 9 8 7 6 5 4 3 2 1

ISBN 978-0-00-822306-9

All rights reserved. No part of this publication may be reproduced, stored in a retrieval system, or transmitted in any form by any means, electronic, mechanical, photocopying, recording or otherwise, without the prior written permission of the Publisher or a licence permitting restricted copying in the United Kingdom issues by the Copyright Licensing Agency Ltd., 90 Tottenham Court Road, London W1T 4LP.

British Library Cataloguing in Publication Data

A catalogue record for this publication is available from the British Library.

Publishing Director: Lee Newman
Publishing Manager: Helen Doran
Senior Editor: Hannah Dove
Project Manager: Emily Hooton
Authors: Sarah Snashall and Chris Whitney
Development Editors: Robert Anderson and Sarah Snashall
Copy-editor: Tanya Solomons
Proofreader: Tracy Thomas
Cover design and artwork: Amparo Barrera and Ken Vail Graphic Design
Internal design concept: Amparo Barrera
Typesetter: Ken Vail Graphic Design
Illustrations: Alberto Saichann (Beehive Illustration)
Production Controller: Rachel Weaver

Printed and bound by CPI Group (UK) Ltd, Croydon, CR0 4YY

Acknowledgements

The publishers wish to thank the following for permission to reproduce content. Every effort has been made to trace copyright holders and to obtain their permission for the use of copyright materials. The publishers will gladly receive any information enabling them to rectify any error or omission at the first opportunity.

Penguin Books Ltd and HarperCollins Publishers for extracts on pages 23-24 from *Goodnight Mister Tom* by Michelle Magorian, Puffin, 1981, copyright © Michelle Magorian, 1981, 1982. Reproduced by permission of Penguin Books Ltd and HarperCollins Publishers; Wes Magee for the poems on pages 25-56 "Simile poem" and "What is ... The Sun?" from *The Witch's Brew and Other Poems* by Wes Magee, Cambridge University Press, 1989. Reproduced by permission of the author Wes Magee; United Agents for the poem on pages 33-34 "Kenneth" by Wendy Cope, copyright © Wendy Cope 2015. Reproduced by permission of United Agents www.unitedagents.co.uk on behalf of Wendy Cope; and Penguin Random House Canada for extracts on pages 38-39 from *Underground to Canada* by Barbara Smucker, copyright © Clarke, Irwin & Company Limited, Toronto/Vancouver, 1977. Reproduced by permission of Penguin Random House Canada Young Readers, a division of Penguin Random House Canada Limited.

Contents

About Treasure House 4

Support, embed and challenge 12

Assessment 13

Support with teaching composition 14

Delivering the 2014 National Curriculum for English 15

Unit 1: Writing persuasive texts 21

Unit 2: Continuing a story 23

Unit 3: Similes and metaphors 25

Unit 4: Stage directions 27

Unit 5: Different kinds of recount (1) 29

Unit 6: Different kinds of recount (2) 31

Unit 7: Writing narrative poems 33

Review unit 1 35

Unit 8: Using linking words and phrases 36

Unit 9: Character perspectives 38

Unit 10: Dialogue 40

Unit 11: Writing a persuasive letter 42

Unit 12: Writing factual reports and opinion pieces 45

Unit 13: Writing for an audience 47

Unit 14: Describing settings 49

Review unit 2 51

Unit 15: Conveying atmosphere 52

Unit 16: Précising longer texts 54

Unit 17: Using organisational features 56

Unit 18: Building cohesion 58

Unit 19: Funny stories 60

Unit 20: List poems 62

Review unit 3 64

Photocopiable resources 65

About Treasure House

Treasure House is a comprehensive and flexible bank of books and online resources for teaching the English curriculum. The Treasure House series offers two different pathways: one covering each English strand discretely (Skills Focus Pathway) and one integrating texts and the strands to create a programme of study (Integrated English Pathway). This Teacher's Guide is part of the Skills Focus Pathway.

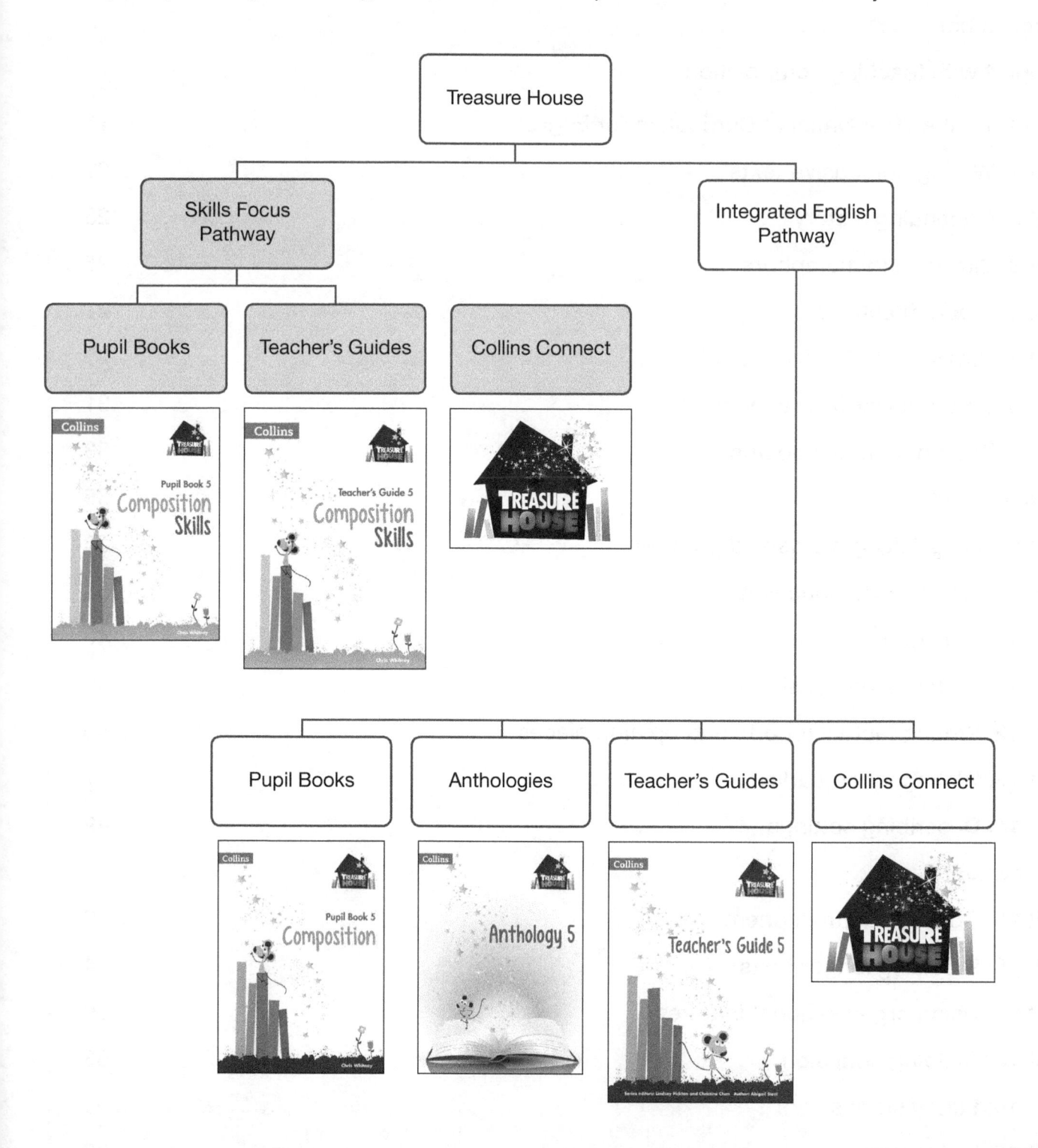

```
Treasure House
├── Skills Focus Pathway
│   ├── Pupil Books
│   ├── Teacher's Guides
│   └── Collins Connect
└── Integrated English Pathway
    ├── Pupil Books
    ├── Anthologies
    ├── Teacher's Guides
    └── Collins Connect
```

About Treasure House

1. Skills Focus

The Skills Focus Pupil Books and Teacher's Guides for all four strands (Comprehension; Spelling; Composition; and Vocabulary, Grammar and Punctuation) allow you to teach each curriculum area in a targeted way. Each unit in the Pupil Book is mapped directly to the statutory requirements of the National Curriculum. Each Teacher's Guide provides step-by-step instructions to guide you through the Pupil Book activities and digital Collins Connect resources for each competency. With a clear focus on skills and clearly-listed curriculum objectives you can select the appropriate resources to support your lessons.

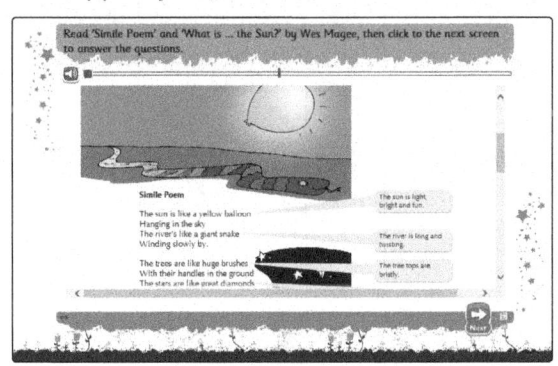

2. Integrated English

Alternatively, the Integrated English pathway offers a complete programme of genre-based teaching sequences. There is one Teacher's Guide and one Anthology for each year group. Each Teacher's Guide provides 15 teaching sequences focused on different genres of text such as fairy tales, letters and newspaper articles. The Anthologies contain the classic texts, fiction, non-fiction and poetry required for each sequence. Each sequence also weaves together all four dimensions of the National Curriculum for English – Comprehension; Spelling; Composition; and Vocabulary, Grammar and Punctuation – into a complete English programme. The Pupil Books and Collins Connect provide targeted explanation of key points and practice activities organised by strand. This programme provides 30 weeks of teaching inspiration.

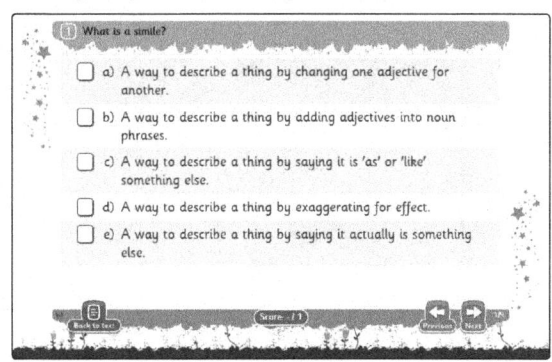

Other components

Handwriting Books, Handwriting Workbooks, Word Books and the online digital resources on Collins Connect are suitable for use with both pathways.

About Treasure House

Treasure House Skills Focus Teacher's Guides

Year	Comprehension	Composition	Vocabulary, Grammar and Punctuation	Spelling
1	978-0-00-822290-1	978-0-00-822302-1	978-0-00-822296-3	978-0-00-822308-3
2	978-0-00-822291-8	978-0-00-822303-8	978-0-00-822297-0	978-0-00-822309-0
3	978-0-00-822292-5	978-0-00-822304-5	978-0-00-822298-7	978-0-00-822310-6
4	978-0-00-822293-2	978-0-00-822305-2	978-0-00-822299-4	978-0-00-822311-3
5	978-0-00-822294-9	978-0-00-822306-9	978-0-00-822300-7	978-0-00-822312-0
6	978-0-00-822295-6	978-0-00-822307-6	978-0-00-822301-4	978-0-00-822313-7

About Treasure House

Inside the Skills Focus Teacher's Guides

The teaching notes in each unit in the Teacher's Guide provide you with subject information or background, a range of whole class and differentiated activities including photocopiable resource sheets and links to the Pupil Book and the online Collins Connect activities.

Each **Overview** provides clear objectives for each lesson tied into the new curriculum, links to the other relevant components and a list of any additional resources required.

Teaching overview provides a brief introduction to the specific skill concept or text type and some pointers on how to approach it.

Support, embed & challenge supports a mastery approach with activities provided at three levels.

Introduce the concept/text provides 5–10 minutes of preliminary discussion points or class/group activities to get the pupils engaged in the lesson focus and set out any essential prior learning.

Pupil practice gives guidance and the answers to each of the three sections in the Pupil Book: *Get started*, *Try these* and *Now try these*.

Homework / Additional activities lists ideas for classroom or homework activities, and relevant activities from Collins Connect.

Two photocopiable **resource** worksheets per unit provide differentiated support for the writing task in each lesson. They are designed to be used with the activities in support or embed sections.

About Treasure House

Treasure House Skills Focus Pupil Books

There are four Skills Focus Pupil Books for each year group, based on the four dimensions of the National Curriculum for English: Comprehension; Spelling; Composition; and Vocabulary, Grammar and Punctuation. The Pupil Books provide a child-friendly introduction to each subject and a range of initial activities for independent pupil-led learning. A Review unit for each term assesses pupils' progress.

Year	Comprehension	Composition	Vocabulary, Grammar and Punctuation	Spelling
1	978-0-00-823634-2	978-0-00-823646-5	978-0-00-823640-3	978-0-00-823652-6
2	978-0-00-823635-9	978-0-00-823647-2	978-0-00-823641-0	978-0-00-823653-3
3	978-0-00-823636-6	978-0-00-823648-9	978-0-00-823642-7	978-0-00-823654-0
4	978-0-00-823637-3	978-0-00-823649-6	978-0-00-823643-4	978-0-00-823655-7
5	978-0-00-823638-0	978-0-00-823650-2	978-0-00-823644-1	978-0-00-823656-4
6	978-0-00-823639-7	978-0-00-823651-9	978-0-00-823645-8	978-0-00-823657-1

About Treasure House

Inside the Skills Focus Pupil Books

Comprehension

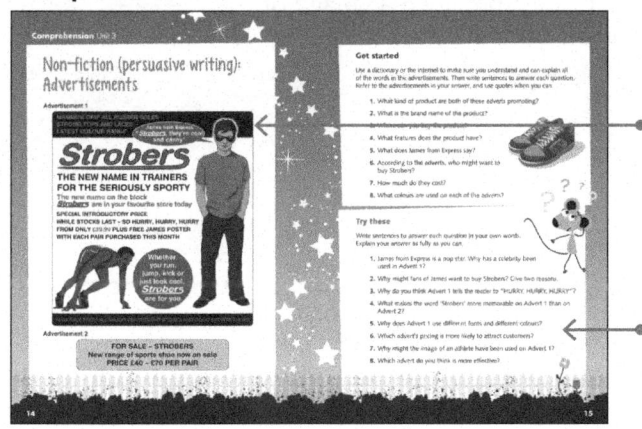

Includes high-quality text extracts covering poetry, prose, traditional tales, playscripts and non-fiction.

Pupils retrieve and record information, learn to draw inferences from texts and increase their familiarity with a wide range of literary genres.

Composition

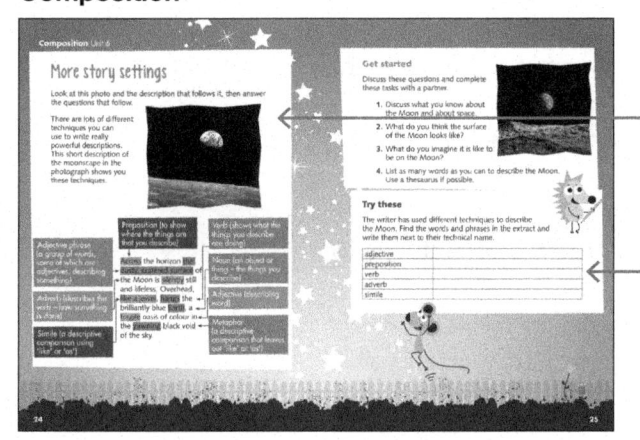

Includes high-quality, annotated text extracts as models for different types of writing.

Children learn how to write effectively and for a purpose.

Vocabulary, Grammar and Punctuation

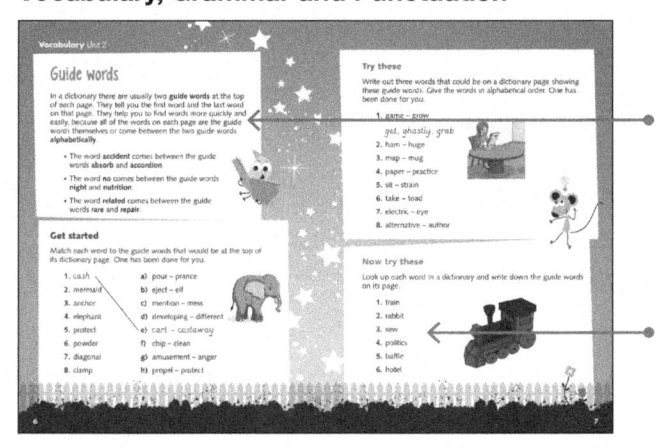

Develops children's knowledge and understanding of grammar and punctuation skills.

A rule is introduced and explained. Children are given lots of opportunities to practise using it.

Spelling

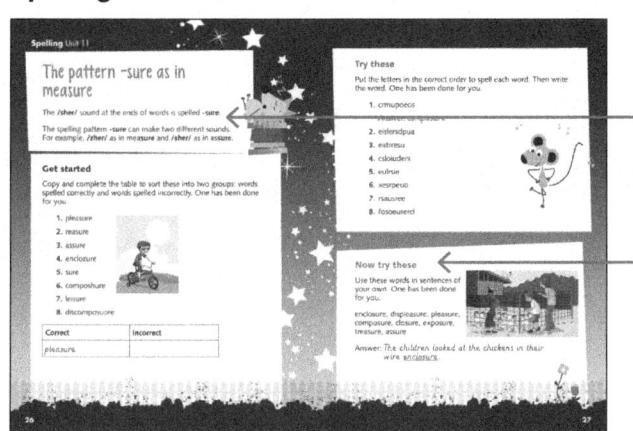

Spelling rules are introduced and explained.

Practice is provided for spotting and using the spelling rules, correcting misspelt words and using the words in context.

About Treasure House

Treasure House on Collins Connect

Digital resources for Treasure House are available on Collins Connect which provides a wealth of interactive activities. Treasure House is organised into six core areas on Collins Connect:

- Comprehension
- Spelling
- Composition
- Vocabulary, Grammar and Punctuation
- The Reading Attic
- Teacher's Guides and Anthologies.

For most units in the Skills Focus Pupil Books, there is an accompanying Collins Connect unit focused on the same teaching objective. These fun, independent activities can be used for initial pupil-led learning, or for further practice using a different learning environment. Either way, with Collins Connect, you have a wealth of questions to help children embed their learning.

Treasure House on Collins Connect is available via subscription at connect.collins.co.uk

Features of Treasure House on Collins Connect

The digital resources enhance children's comprehension, spelling, composition, and vocabulary, grammar, punctuation skills through providing:

- a bank of varied and engaging interactive activities so children can practise their skills independently
- audio support to help children access the texts and activities
- auto-mark functionality so children receive instant feedback and have the opportunity to repeat tasks.

Teachers benefit from useful resources and time-saving tools including:

- teacher-facing materials such as audio and explanations for front-of-class teaching or pupil-led learning
- lesson starter videos for some Composition units
- downloadable teaching notes for all online activities
- downloadable teaching notes for Skills Focus and Integrated English pathways
- the option to assign homework activities to your classes
- class records to monitor progress.

Comprehension

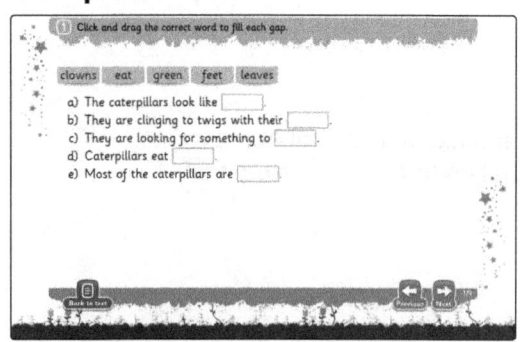

- Includes high-quality text extracts covering poetry, prose, traditional tales, playscripts and non-fiction.
- Audio function supports children to access the text and the activities

Composition

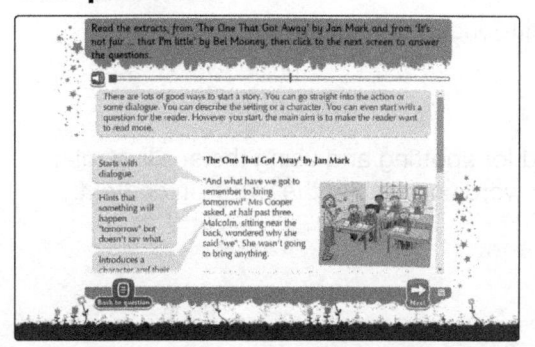

- Activities support children to develop and build more sophisticated sentence structures.
- Every unit ends with a longer piece of writing that can be submitted to the teacher for marking.

About Treasure House

Vocabulary, Grammar and Punctuation

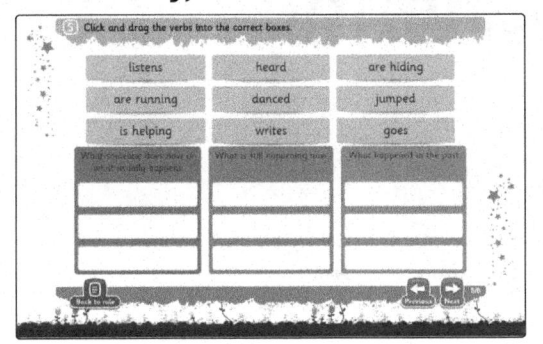

- Fun, practical activities develop children's knowledge and understanding of grammar and punctuation skills.
- Each skill is reinforced with a huge, varied bank of practice questions.

Spelling

- Fun, practical activities develop children's knowledge and understanding of each spelling rule.
- Each rule is reinforced with a huge, varied bank of practice questions.
- Children spell words using an audio prompt, write their own sentences and practise spelling using Look Say Cover Write Check.

Reading Attic

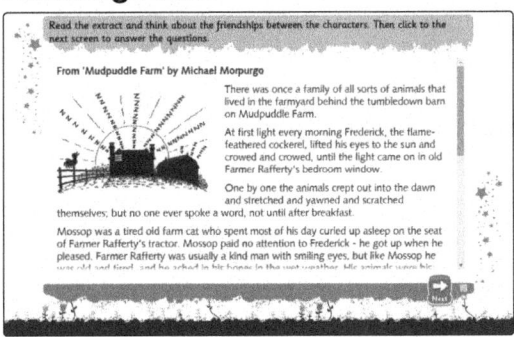

- Children's love of reading is nurtured with texts from exciting children's authors including Michael Bond, David Walliams and Michael Morpurgo.
- Lesson sequences accompany the texts, with drama opportunities and creative strategies for engaging children with key themes, characters and plots.
- Whole-book projects encourage reading for pleasure.

Treasure House Digital Teacher's Guides and Anthologies

The teaching sequences and anthology texts for each year group are included as a flexible bank of resources.

The teaching notes for each skill strand and year group are also included on Collins Connect.

Support, embed and challenge

Treasure House provides comprehensive, detailed differentiation at three levels to ensure that all children are able to access achievement. It is important that children master the basic skills before they go further in their learning. Children may make progress towards the standard at different speeds, with some not reaching it until the very end of the year.

In the Teacher's Guide, Support, Embed and Challenge sections allow teachers to keep the whole class focussed with no child left behind. Two photocopiable resources per unit offer additional material linked to the Support, Embed or Challenge sections.

Support

The Support section offers simpler or more scaffolded activities that will help learners who have not yet grasped specific concepts covered. Background information may also be provided to help children to contextualise learning. This enables children to make progress so that they can keep up with the class.

To help with children's composition skills, activities are broken down into smaller steps, for example, children draw pictures, write plans or complete templates before writing sentences.

If you have a teaching assistant, you may wish to ask him or her to help children work through these activities. You might then ask children who have completed these activities to progress to other more challenging tasks found in the Embed or Challenge sections – or you may decide more practice of the basics is required. Collins Connect can provide further activities.

Embed

The Embed section includes activities to embed learning and is aimed at those who children who are working at the expected standard. It ensures that learners have understood key teaching objectives for the age-group. These activities could be used by the whole class or groups, and most are appropriate for both teacher-led and independent work.

In Composition, children can practise their writing skills using templates, plans and prompts allowing them to write a variety of text-types at the required standard.

Challenge

The Challenge section provides additional tasks, questions or activities that will push children who have mastered the concept without difficulty. This keeps children motivated and allows them to gain a greater depth of understanding. You may wish to give these activities to fast finishers to work through independently.

In Composition, children's writing skills can be enhanced with the freer activities in the Challenge section, for example, they may write an alternative ending to a story, retell a story in their own words or think about a story from another perspective. Children can demonstrate more advanced use of vocabulary and manipulate grammar more accurately through these tasks.

Assessment

Teacher's Guide

There are opportunities for assessment throughout the Treasure House series. The teaching notes in Treasure House Teacher's Guides offer ideas for questions, informal assessment and spelling tests.

Pupil Book Review units

Each Pupil Book has three Review units designed as a quick formative assessment tool for the end of each term. Questions assess the work that has been covered over the previous units. These review units will provide you with an informal way of measuring your pupils' progress. You may wish to use these as Assessment for Learning to help you and your pupils to understand where they are in their learning journey.

In Treasure House, there is a strong focus on genres of texts that widen children's knowledge of writing for different purposes and audiences. In Composition, the review units allow children to demonstrate what they know in independent tasks. Vocabulary, grammar and punctuation can be assessed through their writing as well as their understanding of a genre.

Assessment in Collins Connect

Activities on Collins Connect can also be used for effective assessment. Activities with auto-marking mean that if children answer incorrectly, they can make another attempt helping them to analyse their own work for mistakes. Homework activities can also be assigned to classes through Collins Connect. At the end of activities, children can select a smiley face to indicate how they found the task giving you useful feedback on any gaps in knowledge.

Class records on Collins Connect allow you to get an overview of children's progress with several features. You can choose to view records by unit, pupil or strand. By viewing detailed scores, you can view pupils' scores question by question in a clear table-format to help you establish areas where there might be particular strengths and weaknesses both class-wide and for individuals.

If you wish, you can also set mastery judgements (mastery achieved and exceeded, mastery achieved, mastery not yet achieved) to help see where your children need more help.

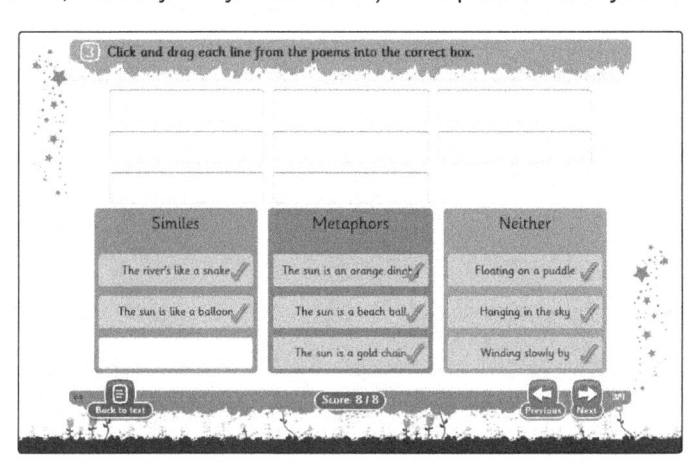

Support with teaching composition

Composition is one of the four core dimensions of the National Curriculum for English. Within the teaching of English, the aim is to ensure that all pupils write clearly, accurately and coherently, adapting their language and style in and for a range of contexts, purposes and audiences.

Effective composition involves forming, articulating and communicating ideas, and then organising them coherently for a reader. This requires clarity and an awareness of the audience, purpose and context. All children can be helped towards better writing if shown how to generate and organise ideas appropriately and how to then transfer them successfully from plan to page. In addition, pupils need to be taught how to plan, revise and evaluate their writing. These aspects of writing have been incorporated into the Treasure House Composition Skills strand.

Throughout the primary years, we want pupils to have opportunities to write for a range of real purposes and audiences as part of their work across the curriculum. These purposes and audiences should underpin the decisions about the form the writing should take, such as a narrative, an explanation or a description. We want pupils to develop positive attitudes towards their writing and stamina for it by writing narratives about personal experiences and those of others, by writing about real events, by writing poetry and by writing for different purposes.

Pupils also need to be taught to monitor whether their own writing makes sense. They should also understand, through being shown, the skills and processes essential for writing: the generation of ideas, initial drafting, and re-reading to check that the meaning is clear.

Treasure House Composition Skills Teacher's Guides provide extensive notes and guidance for teaching a range of genres and text types. The integrated pupil books provide opportunities for pupils to plan, draft and edit their writing. Each unit is linked to an extract of quality text from which the teaching ideas are taken.

Delivering the 2014 National Curriculum for English

Unit	Title	Treasure House Resources	Collins Connect	English Programme of Study
1	Writing persuasive texts	• Composition Skills Pupil Book 5, Unit 1, pages 4–7 • Composition Skills Teacher's Guide 5 – Unit 1, pages 21–22 – Photocopiable Unit 1, Resource 1: Planning my persuasive argument, page 65 – Photocopiable Unit 1, Resource 2: My persuasive argument, page 66	Collins Connect Treasure House Composition Year 5, Unit 1	**Writing:** Identifying the audience for and purpose of the writing, selecting the appropriate form and using other similar writing as models for their own. Noting and developing initial ideas, drawing on reading and research where necessary. Selecting appropriate grammar and vocabulary, understanding how such choices can change and enhance meaning. Using a wide range of devices to build cohesion within and across paragraphs.
2	Continuing a story	• Composition Skills Pupil Book 5, Unit 2, pages 8–11 • Composition Skills Teacher's Guide 5 – Unit 2, pages 23–24 – Photocopiable Unit 2, Resource 1: Planning the next episode, page 67 – Photocopiable Unit 2, Resource 2: Writing the next episode, page 68	Collins Connect Treasure House Composition Year 5, Unit 2	**Writing:** Identifying the audience for and purpose of the writing, selecting the appropriate form and using other similar writing as models for their own. Noting and developing initial ideas, drawing on reading. Planning their writing by considering how authors have developed characters and settings in what pupils have read, listened to or seen performed. Drafting and writing by selecting appropriate grammar and vocabulary, understanding how such choices can change and enhance meaning. Drafting and writing by describing settings, characters and atmosphere and integrating dialogue to convey character and advance the action.
3	Similes and metaphors	• Composition Skills Pupil Book 5, Unit 3, pages 12–15 • Composition Skills Teacher's Guide 5 – Unit 3, pages 25–26 – Photocopiable Unit 3, Resource 1: My simile poem, page 69 – Photocopiable Unit 3, Resource 2: My metaphor poem, page 70	Collins Connect Treasure House Composition Year 5, Unit 3	**Writing:** Identifying the audience for and purpose of the writing, selecting the appropriate form and using other similar writing as models for their own. Drafting and writing by selecting appropriate vocabulary, understanding how such choices can change and enhance meaning. Evaluating and editing by assessing the effectiveness of their own and others' writing.
4	Stage directions	• Composition Skills Pupil Book 5, Unit 4, pages 16–19 • Composition Skills Teacher's Guide 5 – Unit 4, pages 27–28 – Photocopiable Unit 4, Resource 1: Stage directions, page 71 – Photocopiable Unit 4, Resource 2: The glass slipper, page 72	Collins Connect Treasure House Composition Year 5, Unit 4	**Writing:** Identifying the audience for and purpose of the writing, selecting the appropriate form and using other similar writing as models for their own. Noting and developing initial ideas, drawing on reading and research where necessary. Planning their writing by considering how authors have developed characters and settings in what pupils have read, listened to or seen performed. Drafting and writing by selecting appropriate grammar and vocabulary, understanding how such choices can change and enhance meaning. Describing settings.

5	Different kinds of recount (1)	• Composition Skills Pupil Book 5, Unit 5, pages 20–23
		• Composition Skills Teacher's Guide 5
		  – Unit 5, pages 29–30
		  – Photocopiable Unit 5, Resource 1: Letter to a friend, page 73
		  – Photocopiable Unit 5, Resource 2: Magazine article, page 74
			Collins Connect Treasure House Composition Year 5, Unit 5	**Writing:** Identifying the audience for and purpose of the writing, selecting the appropriate form and using other similar writing as models for their own. Noting and developing initial ideas, drawing on reading and research where necessary.
				Drafting and writing by selecting appropriate grammar and vocabulary, understanding how such choices can change and enhance meaning.

6	Different kinds of recount (2)	• Composition Skills Pupil Book 5, Unit 6, pages 24–27
		• Composition Skills Teacher's Guide 5
		  – Unit 6, pages 31–32
		  – Photocopiable Unit 6, Resource 1: Police report, page 75
		  – Photocopiable Unit 6, Resource 2: Diary entry, page 76
			Collins Connect Treasure House Composition Year 5, Unit 6	**Writing:** Identifying the audience for and purpose of the writing, selecting the appropriate form and using other similar writing as models for their own. Noting and developing initial ideas, drawing on reading and research where necessary.
				Drafting and writing by selecting appropriate grammar and vocabulary, understanding how such choices can change and enhance meaning.
				Using a wide range of devices to build cohesion within and across paragraphs.

7	Writing narrative poems	• Composition Skills Pupil Book 5, Unit 7, pages 28–31
		• Composition Skills Teacher's Guide 5
		  – Unit 7, pages 33–34
		  – Photocopiable Unit 7, Resource 1: Planning my narrative poem, page 77
		  – Photocopiable Unit 7, Resource 2: Writing my narrative poem, page 78
			Collins Connect Treasure House Composition Year 5, Unit 7	**Reading:** Learning a wider range of poetry by heart. Preparing poems to read aloud and to perform showing understanding through intonation, tone and volume so that the meaning is clear to an audience.
				Writing: Identifying the audience for and purpose of the writing, selecting the appropriate form and using other similar writing as models for their own. Noting and developing initial ideas, drawing on reading and research where necessary.
				Planning their writing by considering how authors have developed characters and settings in what pupils have read, listened to or seen performed.
				Drafting and writing by selecting appropriate grammar and vocabulary, understanding how such choices can change and enhance meaning.
				Drafting and writing by describing settings, characters and atmosphere and integrating dialogue to convey character and advance the action.

8	Using linking words and phrases	**Writing:** Identifying the audience for and purpose of the writing, selecting the appropriate form and using other similar writing as models for their own. Noting and developing initial ideas, drawing on reading. Drafting and writing by selecting appropriate grammar and vocabulary, understanding how such choices can change and enhance meaning. Using a wide range of devices to build cohesion within and across paragraphs. Linking ideas across paragraphs using adverbials of time (for example, later), place (for example, nearby) and number (for example, secondly). Evaluating and editing by assessing the effectiveness of their own and others' writing. Proposing changes to vocabulary, grammar and punctuation to enhance effects and clarify meaning.	Collins Connect Treasure House Composition Year 5, Unit 8	• Composition Skills Pupil Book 5, Unit 8, pages 34–36 • Composition Skills Teacher's Guide 5 – Unit 8, pages 36–37 – Photocopiable Unit 8, Resource 1 Adding linking words and phrases, page 79 – Photocopiable Unit 8, Resource 2: My sentences, page 80
9	Character perspectives	**Writing:** Identifying the audience for and purpose of the writing, selecting the appropriate form and using other similar writing as models for their own. Noting and developing initial ideas, drawing on reading. Drafting and writing by selecting appropriate grammar and vocabulary, understanding how such choices can change and enhance meaning. Drafting and writing by describing settings, characters and atmosphere and integrating dialogue to convey character and advance the action.	Collins Connect Treasure House Composition Year 5, Unit 9	• Composition Skills Pupil Book 5, Unit 9, pages 37–40 • Composition Skills Teacher's Guide 5 – Unit 9, pages 38–39 – Photocopiable Unit 9, Resource 1: Goldilocks and Baby Bear, page 81 – Photocopiable Unit 9, Resource 2: A trip to the zoo, page 82
10	Dialogue	**Writing:** Identifying the audience for and purpose of the writing, selecting the appropriate form and using other similar writing as models for their own. Noting and developing initial ideas, drawing on reading and research where necessary. Planning their writing by considering how authors have developed characters and settings in what pupils have read, listened to or seen performed. Drafting and writing by selecting appropriate grammar and vocabulary, understanding how such choices can change and enhance meaning. Drafting and writing by describing settings, characters and atmosphere and integrating dialogue to convey character and advance the action. Vocabulary, grammar and punctuation (from Year 4): Using inverted commas and other punctuation to indicate direct speech.	Collins Connect Treasure House Composition Year 5, Unit 10	• Composition Skills Pupil Book 5, Unit 10, pages 41–44 • Composition Skills Teacher's Guide 5 – Unit 10, pages 40–41 – Photocopiable Unit 10, Resource 1: Plan for a conversation in a shop, page 83 – Photocopiable Unit 10, Resource 2: Dialogue in a shop, page 84

11	Writing a persuasive letter	• Composition Skills Pupil Book 5, Unit 11, pages 45–47 • Composition Skills Teacher's Guide 5 – Unit 11, pages 42–44 – Photocopiable Unit 11, Resource 1: Planning my persuasive letter, page 85 – Photocopiable Unit 11, Resource 2: My persuasive letter, page 86	Collins Connect Treasure House Composition Year 5, Unit 11	**Writing:** Identifying the audience for and purpose of the writing, selecting the appropriate form and using other similar writing as models for their own. Noting and developing initial ideas, drawing on reading and research where necessary. Drafting and writing by selecting appropriate grammar and vocabulary, understanding how such choices can change and enhance meaning. Using a wide range of devices to build cohesion within and across paragraphs. Evaluating and editing by assessing the effectiveness of their own and others' writing.
12	Writing factual reports and opinion pieces	• Composition Skills Pupil Book 5, Unit 12, pages 48–51 • Composition Skills Teacher's Guide 5 – Unit 12, pages 45–46 – Photocopiable Unit 12, Resource 1: My newspaper report, page 87 – Photocopiable Unit 12, Resource 2: My newspaper editorial, page 88	Collins Connect Treasure House Composition Year 5, Unit 12	**Writing:** Identifying the audience for and purpose of the writing, selecting the appropriate form and using other similar writing as models for their own. Noting and developing initial ideas, drawing on reading and research where necessary. Drafting and writing by selecting appropriate grammar and vocabulary, understanding how such choices can change and enhance meaning. Using a wide range of devices to build cohesion within and across paragraphs. Evaluating and editing by assessing the effectiveness of their own and others' writing.
13	Writing for an audience	• Composition Skills Pupil Book 5, Unit 13, pages 52–55 • Composition Skills Teacher's Guide 5 – Unit 13, pages 47–48 – Photocopiable Unit 13, Resource 1: A tale for older children, page 89 – Photocopiable Unit 13, Resource 2: A tale for younger children, page 90	Collins Connect Treasure House Composition Year 5, Unit 13	**Writing:** Identifying the audience for and purpose of the writing, selecting the appropriate form and using other similar writing as models for their own. Noting and developing initial ideas, drawing on reading and research where necessary. Drafting and writing by selecting appropriate grammar and vocabulary, understanding how such choices can change and enhance meaning. Drafting and writing by describing settings, characters and atmosphere and integrating dialogue to convey character and advance the action.
14	Describing settings	• Composition Skills Pupil Book 5, Unit 14, pages 56–58 • Composition Skills Teacher's Guide 5 – Unit 14, pages 49–50 – Photocopiable Unit 14, Resource 1: Planning the description, page 91 – Photocopiable Unit 14, Resource 2: My descriptive paragraph, page 92	Collins Connect Treasure House Composition Year 5, Unit 14	**Writing:** Identifying the audience for and purpose of the writing, selecting the appropriate form and using other similar writing as models for their own. Noting and developing initial ideas, drawing on reading and research where necessary. Planning their writing by considering how authors have developed characters and settings in what pupils have read, listened to or seen performed. Drafting and writing by selecting appropriate grammar and vocabulary, understanding how such choices can change and enhance meaning. Drafting and writing by describing settings, characters and atmosphere and integrating dialogue to convey character and advance the action.

15	Conveying atmosphere	• Composition Skills Pupil Book 5, Unit 15, pages 61–63 • Composition Skills Teacher's Guide 5 – Unit 15, pages 52–53 – Photocopiable Unit 15, Resource 1: Planning the paragraph, page 93 – Photocopiable Unit 15, Resource 2: Conveying atmosphere, page 94	Collins Connect Treasure House Composition Year 5, Unit 15
		Writing: Identifying the audience for and purpose of the writing, selecting the appropriate form and using other similar writing as models for their own. Noting and developing initial ideas, drawing on reading and research where necessary. Planning their writing by considering how authors have developed characters and settings in what pupils have read, listened to or seen performed. Drafting and writing by selecting appropriate grammar and vocabulary, understanding how such choices can change and enhance meaning. Drafting and writing by describing settings, characters and atmosphere and integrating dialogue to convey character and advance the action.		
16	Précising longer texts	• Composition Skills Pupil Book 5, Unit 16, pages 64–68 • Composition Skills Teacher's Guide 5 – Unit 16, pages 54–55 – Photocopiable Unit 16, Resource 1: Mowgli arrives, page 95 – Photocopiable Unit 16, Resource 2: Improving my précis, page 96	
		Writing: Drafting and writing by précising longer passages. Evaluating and editing by assessing the effectiveness of their own and others' writing.		
17	Using organisational features	• Composition Skills Pupil Book 5, Unit 17, pages 69–71 • Composition Skills Teacher's Guide 5 – Unit 17, pages 56–57 – Photocopiable Unit 17, Resource 1: Elements for my Solar System poster, page 97 – Photocopiable Unit 17, Resource 2: Solar System notes, page 98	
		Writing: Noting and developing initial ideas, drawing on reading and research where necessary. Drafting and writing by using further organisational and presentational devices to structure text and to guide the reader (for example, headings, bullet points, underlining).		
18	Building cohesion	• Composition Skills Pupil Book 5, Unit 18, pages 72–73 • Composition Skills Teacher's Guide 5 – Unit 18, pages 58–59 – Photocopiable Unit 18, Resource 1: Useful linking phrases, page 99 – Photocopiable Unit 18, Resource 2: Saturn V rocket launch, page 100	
		Writing: Noting and developing initial ideas, drawing on reading and research where necessary. Drafting and writing by selecting appropriate grammar and vocabulary, understanding how such choices can change and enhance meaning. Using a wide range of devices to build cohesion within and across paragraphs.		

19	Funny stories	• Composition Skills Pupil Book 5, Unit 19, pages 74–78
		• Composition Skills Teacher's Guide 5
		  – Unit 19, pages 60–61
		  – Photocopiable Unit 19, Resource 1: Toad flying high, page 101
		  – Photocopiable Unit 19, Resource 2: Planning a new adventure for Toad, page 102
			Writing: Drafting and writing by describing settings, characters and atmosphere and integrating dialogue to convey character and advance the action.

20	List poems	• Composition Skills Pupil Book 5, Unit 20, pages 79–81
		• Composition Skills Teacher's Guide 5
		  – Unit 20, pages 62–63
		  – Photocopiable Unit 20, Resource 1: Snowy day, page 103
		  – Photocopiable Unit 20, Resource 2: Scary vocabulary, page 104
			Writing: Identifying the audience for and purpose of the writing, selecting the appropriate form and using other similar writing as models for their own. Drafting and writing by selecting appropriate grammar and vocabulary, understanding how such choices can change and enhance meaning.

	All units	The following statutory requirements can be covered throughout the programme:
		Pupils should be taught to:
		• Evaluate and edit by:
		  – ensuring the consistent and correct use of tense throughout a piece of writing
		  – ensuring correct subject and verb agreement when using singular and plural, distinguishing between the language of speech and writing and choosing the appropriate register
		• proof-read for spelling and punctuation errors
		• perform their own compositions, using appropriate intonation, volume, and movement so that meaning is clear.	

Unit 1: Writing persuasive texts

Overview

English curriculum objectives

Writing – composition

Year 5 children should be taught to plan their writing by:

- identifying the audience for and purpose of the writing, selecting the appropriate form and using other similar writing as models for their own
- noting and developing initial ideas, drawing on reading [...] where necessary.

Year 5 children should be taught to draft and write by:

- selecting appropriate grammar and vocabulary, understanding how such choices can change and enhance meaning
- using a wide range of devices to build cohesion within and across paragraphs.

Building towards

Children will consider the persuasive techniques used by an example of an editorial article before planning and writing their own persuasive text.

Treasure house resources

- Composition Skills Pupil Book 5, Unit 1, pages 4–7
- Collins Connect Treasure House Year 5, Unit 1
- Photocopiable Unit 1, Resource 1: Planning my persuasive argument, page 65
- Photocopiable Unit 1, Resource 2: My persuasive argument, page 66

Additional resources

- Persuasive leaflets, for example, leaflets designed to persuade people to visit a tourist attraction
- Charity manifestos – where well-researched and articulated opinions can often be found
- Biased argument articles from magazines and newspapers – print or online for contrast and comparison

Introduction

Teaching overview

This unit focuses on expressing a point of view. The unit is based on an editorial article that exemplifies the text-type features. The unit focuses in particular on ordering, structuring and connecting information in order to present a well-informed and articulate discussion. Children consider these skills and move on to plan and write their own biased or persuasive argument on a topic of their choice.

Introduce the concept

Start the lesson by asking children if they have ever witnessed or been involved in a situation where there were two opposing views to something. Point out that when we write an article voicing both opinions it is called a 'balanced discussion', but when we write giving only one opinion it is called a 'biased discussion'. Show children examples of editorial articles from newspapers and magazines where the editor gives a biased opinion. Charity manifestos can also be a rich source for well-researched and articulated opinions. To help children begin to express their own opinions and understand what it is like to voice those opinions, you may wish to watch one or two children's current affairs programmes.

You may need to do some revision of conjunctive adverbs (connectives) (for example, therefore, thus, yet, moreover) and their key role in linking sentences (and the ideas they contain) together.

Unit 1: Writing persuasive texts

Pupil practice

Pupil Book pages 4–7

Get started
Children work with a partner and discuss any times when they had to try to persuade someone to do something, explaining their arguments and strategies.

Try these
Children answer questions from the text.

Answers

1. The main point is the opinion that the council should pay for more after-school clubs. [1 mark]
2. The main point is summed up in the first sentence. [1 mark]
3. Supporting points add information and evidence to support the main point. [1 mark]
4. The main point is stated in the first sentence and supporting points are organised into one point per paragraph. [1 mark]
5. A balanced discussion views all sides of an issue. [1 mark]
6. The aim of a biased discussion is to persuade the reader to take the writer's point of view. [1 mark]
7. A conclusion should come at the end of any discussion. [1 mark]
8. Connectives show relationships between statements. [1 mark]
9. Examples of connectives: a further reason, furthermore, therefore [1 mark for each]
10. Paragraph 1: This newspaper takes the opinion that the council should pay for more after-school clubs for young people.
    Paragraph 2: There aren't many places where young people can play safely.
    Paragraph 3: The clubs could provide a quiet corner for doing homework.
    Paragraph 4: Clubs would help parents who go to work and can't collect children at the time school finishes.
    Paragraph 5: Conclusion: it would be money well spent. [1 mark per sentence]

Now try these
Children should consider any issues at school that are important to them or that they feel strongly about. They plan a biased or persuasive argument.

Suggested answers

1. The plan should contain: a statement of the main point of the argument; paragraphs that each present a supporting point; notes on a valid conclusion.
2. The full article should relate to the plan, and arguments must have a main point backed up by supporting points. There should be a conclusion at the end. Writing must be in full sentences and paragraphs and include conjunctive adverbs.

You may wish to use the activities and photocopiables in **Support and Embed** to give differentiated support with the writing task in **Now try these**.

Support, embed & challenge

Support
Ask the children to plan their persuasive argument based on an issue they feel strongly about. Unit 1 Resource 1: Planning my persuasive argument supports them with this. Ask the children to use their notes to verbally argue their point.

Embed
Ask the children to write their persuasive argument in full. They are reminded what to include through the checklist provided in Unit 1 Resource 2: My persuasive argument.

Challenge
Ask the children to consider the same issue as in **Now try these** but write a balanced argument giving two or more points of view.

Homework / Additional activities

Persuading your family
Ask the children to write a letter to someone in their family persuading them to do something or to give them something.

Collins Connect: Unit 1
Ask the children to complete Unit 1 (See Teach → Year 5 → Composition → Unit 1).

Unit 2: Continuing a story

Overview

English curriculum objectives

Writing – composition

Year 5 children should be taught to plan their writing by:

- selecting the appropriate form and using other similar writing as models for their own
- noting and developing initial ideas, drawing on reading
- in writing narratives, considering how authors have developed characters and settings in what children have read.

Year 5 children should be taught to draft and write by:

- selecting appropriate grammar and vocabulary, understanding how such choices can change and enhance meaning
- in narratives, describing settings, characters and atmosphere and integrating dialogue to convey character and advance the action.

Building towards

Children will continue a story by writing the next episode.

Treasure house resources

- Composition Skills Pupil Book 5, Unit 2, pages 8–11
- Collins Connect Treasure House Year 5, Unit 2
- Photocopiable Unit 2, Resource 1: Planning the next episode, page 67
- Photocopiable Unit 2, Resource 2: Writing the next episode, page 68

Additional resources

- Copies of *Goodnight Mister Tom* for reading after the unit is completed
- Film version of *Goodnight Mister Tom* (1998) for possible viewing after the unit is completed
- A selection of further books by Michelle Magorian for children to browse and read after the unit is completed

Introduction

Teaching overview

This unit focuses on continuing a story. The unit includes an extract from *Goodnight Mister Tom* (1981) by the English writer Michelle Magorian (born 1947), with notes on the features of this genre and the writing skills employed by the author. The unit also looks at the author's combination of description, dialogue and character. Children consider the characters in the extract, in particular the Billeting Officer, and think about how the plot might develop. They then write a fictional scene that could follow the extract, using the same style as the author and noting the techniques used in the unit.

Goodnight Mister Tom is the story of a boy evacuee during the Second World War who leaves London to live with a kindly elderly recluse, the Mister Tom of the title. There may be links with the Key Stage 2 History curriculum.

Introduce the concept

It may be helpful for children to understand the historical context of *Goodnight Mister Tom* and what is meant by an 'evacuee' before attempting the unit. Once it is established, the class could be asked to discuss what they know about narrative plot from previous work and specifically how, in stories, each succeeding episode typically builds on or arises out of the previous ones. You could try an activity in which the children are given a part of a plot summary, read the opening paragraphs of a short story or perhaps watch the beginning of a short film, and are then asked: 'What do you think happens next in the plot?'

At the end of the lesson, you might like to read the next part of *Goodnight Mister Tom* or watch a clip of the episode from the film version.

Unit 2: Continuing a story

Pupil practice
Pupil Book pages 8–11

Get started
Children work with a partner to share their knowledge of the evacuation of children in the Second World War. They research information and make notes.

Try these
Children make notes about the two characters, referring to the text extract. Award one mark for each point.

Notes should include some or all of the following:

Thomas Oakley	William Beech
in his sixties	small; thin and sickly-looking, pale with limp, sandy hair and dull grey eyes
healthy, robust, stocky build	quiet and shy
head of thick white hair	
like a towering giant with skin like coarse, wrinkled brown paper and a voice like thunder	
speaks abruptly and impatiently	

Now try these
1. Children answer questions about the Billeting Officer and the remaining evacuees.

Answers
a. She is a middle-aged woman, wearing a green coat and felt hat. [1 mark]
b. Her job as Billeting Officer is to find homes for the evacuees. [1 mark]
c. She finds her job hard work and stressful (she looks harassed). [1 mark]
d. She is taking the other evacuees to the village hall. [1 mark]
e. Other villagers will come to choose a child to take home. [1 mark]
f. Many of them were filthy and very poorly clad. Only a handful of them had a blazer or a coat. One tiny dark-haired girl in the front was hanging firmly on to a new teddy bear. [1 mark]
g. They all looked bewildered and exhausted. [1 mark]

2. Children should consider what might happen next to the Billeting Officer and the remaining evacuees and write the next episode. The episode should be written in the past tense and include correctly punctuated dialogue.

You may wish to use the activities and photocopiables in **Support and Embed** to give differentiated support with the writing task in **Now try these**.

Support, embed & challenge

Support
Encourage the children to use role play and hot seating to investigate the emotions of the other evacuees before using Unit 2 Resource 1: Planning the next episode to make a storyboard of their scene, adding speech bubbles if possible. Encourage them to write some of their story.

Embed
Ask the children to write the next episode in the story, combining narrative and dialogue. The checklist in Unit 2 Resource 2: Writing the next episode supports them with this.

Challenge
Ask the children to rewrite the extract, this time from the point of view of Tom or William (using the first person). They should use dialogue to show character and advance the action.

Homework / Additional activities

Writing home
Ask the children to write a letter home from one of the evacuees to their family in London telling them about their journey to the countryside and where they are now.

Collins Connect: Unit 2
Ask the children to complete Unit 2 (See Teach → Year 5 → Composition → Unit 2).

Unit 3: Similes and metaphors

Overview

English curriculum objectives

Writing – composition

Year 5 children should be taught to plan their writing by selecting the appropriate form and using other similar writing as models for their own.

Year 5 children should be taught to draft and write by selecting appropriate vocabulary, understanding how such choices can change and enhance meaning.

Year 5 children should be taught to evaluate and edit by assessing the effectiveness of others' writing.

Non-statutory guidance for Key Stage 2

Children should demonstrate understanding of figurative language.

Building towards

Children will write their own poem using simile and metaphor based on the structure in the poems by Wes Magee.

Treasure house resources

- Composition Skills Pupil Book 5, Unit 3, pages 12–15
- Collins Connect Treasure House Year 5, Unit 3
- Photocopiable Unit 3, Resource 1: My simile poem, page 69
- Photocopiable Unit 3, Resource 2: My metaphor poem, page 70

Additional resources

- Collections of poetry by Wes Magee, in book form or online
- Recording of Wes Magee reading his poems available for small fee from the Poetry Archive
- A collection of poems containing simile and metaphor for children to browse and read

Introduction

Teaching overview

This unit focuses on similes and metaphors. The unit includes two poems, 'Simile Poem' and 'What is … the Sun?' both by the English poet Wes Magee (born 1939), to exemplify the writing skills involved and to provide a stimulus for children's own writing. The definitions of simile and metaphor are provided, and children practise differentiating between the two. They analyse the poetic effects of some of the examples from the poems. Children write their own similes and metaphors, and finish by creating a poem based on one of the stimulus poems.

Introduce the concept

Ask the class to give a definition of a simile. Take feedback and provide the children with sentence frames showing the two main simile types: 'as _____ as a _____' (for example, 'As slow as a tortoise') and 'The _____ is like a _____' (for example, 'The sun is like a yellow ball bouncing in the sky'). Ask children to make suggestions for filling in the gaps with nouns or noun phrases. This could be turned into a fun game by asking one child to suggest the first noun and another to suggest the comparison. Encourage children to be as inventive and imaginative as they can – the point is to make the similes as fresh and vivid as possible.

Move on to give an example of a metaphor: 'The night sky is a velvet curtain' or 'He's standing at the foot of the hill'. Ask for the name of this poetic device and explain that, while a simile compares two things by saying one thing is *like* another, a metaphor compares two things by saying one thing *is actually* the other. Use a sentence frame 'The _____ is a _____' and repeat the activity above.

Provide images such as the night sky, the moon, the sea: children work in pairs to write a sentence about these images using both a simile and a metaphor. They share them with the class.

Give each table of children a selection of poems with similes and metaphors to browse through. Ask them to choose one for a volunteer to read to the rest of the class.

Unit 3: Similes and metaphors

Pupil practice

Pupil Book pages 12–15

Get started
Children work with a partner and discuss any similes and metaphors that are known to them. They make a list of similes and add their own.

Possible Answers

as brave as a lion; as quiet as a mouse; as quick as a flash; sleep like a log …

Try these
The children read the poems and complete a table, adding similes and metaphors found in the two poems. Award 1 mark per correct answer.

Answers

Similes	Metaphors
The sun is like a yellow balloon	The sun is an orange dinghy
The river's like a giant snake	It is a gold chain
The trees are like huge bushes	It is a yellow beach ball
The stars are like great diamonds	It is a red thumb print
	It is the gold top from a milk bottle

Now try these
Children complete a table, adding their own noun phrases to describe an object. They use similes in one table and metaphors in another. They add an action to say what the thing the object is compared to is doing. They move on to write their own poem using similes and metaphors.

1. The similes and metaphors should be relevant and complete, with an appropriate action.
2. Their poem should follow the structure of the two poems in the extract.

You may wish to use the activities and photocopiables in **Support and Embed** to give differentiated support with the writing task in **Now try these** question 2.

Support, embed & challenge

Support
Ask these children to focus on writing a simile poem about clouds. Unit 3 Resource 1: My simile poem provides structured support for both the planning and the writing stage of this task.

Embed
Ask the children to think of metaphors to describe their chosen topic, choosing from Clouds, Snow or Friends. They can use the structure provided in Unit 3 Resource 2: My metaphor poem.

Challenge
Ask the children to write a prose description of a story setting of their choice, using both simile and metaphor to paint a vivid picture.

Homework / Additional activities

What are your family like?
Ask the children to write one simile per person as they describe members of their family or family pets.

Collins Connect: Unit 3
Ask the children to complete Unit 3 (See Teach → Year 5 → Composition → Unit 3).

Unit 4: Stage directions

Overview

English curriculum objectives

Writing – composition

Year 5 children should be taught to plan their writing by:

- identifying the audience for and purpose of the writing, selecting the appropriate form and using other similar writing as models for their own
- noting and developing initial ideas, drawing on reading
- in writing narratives, considering how authors have developed characters and settings in what children have read.

Year 5 children should be taught to draft and write by:

- selecting appropriate grammar and vocabulary, understanding how such choices can change and enhance meaning
- in narratives, describing settings.

Notes and guidance (non-statutory)

Children should understand, through being shown, the skills and processes essential for writing.

Building towards

Children will turn a traditional tale into a playscript.

Treasure house resources

- Composition Skills Pupil Book 5, Unit 4, pages 16–19
- Collins Connect Treasure House Year 5, Unit 4
- Photocopiable Unit 4, Resource 1: Stage directions, page 71
- Photocopiable Unit 4, Resource 2: The glass slipper, page 72

Additional resources

- A selection of traditional tales for children to browse and read
- A clip from a recorded dramatic performance, together with a playscript
- Copies of a narrative version of 'Cinderella'

Introduction

Teaching overview

This unit focuses on writing stage directions. The unit includes two scenes from a play, 'The Long Hike', which demonstrate the writing skills involved. The unit looks at identifying the conventions of stage directions and their characteristics, such as descriptive verbs and adverbs. Children are given the opportunity to write their own scene for a play, paying close attention to the stage directions.

Introduce the concept

Before starting the unit it would be useful to show the class an extract from a dramatic presentation such as a recorded theatre performance, a film or a television programme. After watching the performance, ask the children to discuss with a partner how the actors moved and spoke and how they knew how to move and what to say. Take feedback and, if possible, share with children the playscript for the performance they have just seen, exploring in particular the stage directions.

Ask two volunteers to come to the front and read the characters of Harry and John in the extract in the Pupil Book, carrying out as many of the actions as they can. Discuss the stage directions and the layout of the page.

Pupil practice

Pupil Book pages 16–19

Get started

Children work in pairs and share their knowledge of playscripts.

Answers

1. A playscript is the written instructions for performing a story.
2. A scene is a section of a play.
3. The setting is where the play takes place.
4. Information on the setting can be found following the scene number.
5. Rules for writing a playscript:
   - Write the details of where the scene is set at the beginning.
   - Don't use speech marks to show who is speaking.
   - Write the speaker's name followed by a colon to show who speaks each line.

Unit 4: Stage directions

- Start a new line each time a character starts to speak.
- Write stage directions to tell the performers what to do.
- Write the stage directions in the third person and the present tense.
- Put the stage directions in brackets.

Try these
Children answer questions about stage directions.

Answers
1. Stage directions tell the actors: how to enter and exit; how to use any props they have; how to speak the lines; what to do. [1 mark]
2. Stage directions are often enclosed in brackets so that they don't become confused with the dialogue. [1 mark]
3. Stage left refers to the left side of the stage (the audience's right); stage right refers to the right side of the stage (the audience's left). [1 mark]
4. Stage directions should be written in the present tense because they are instructions to the actors. [1 mark]
5. There are a lot of verbs and adverbs in stage directions because they tell the actors what to do and how to do it. [1 mark]
6. Good stage directions are short, clear and direct, and should be written in the present tense. [1 mark]

John	Harry
John and Harry enter stage left [1 mark]	John and Harry enter stage left [1 mark]
John is dragging his feet and looking tired [1 mark]	Harry is walking briskly [1 mark]
(flopping down on the ground) [1 mark]	(looking at the map) [1 mark]
(crossly) [1 mark]	(sitting down next to John) [1 mark]
(sounding worried) [1 mark]	(jumping up quickly) [1 mark]
(getting up slowly) [1 mark]	Harry marches off briskly stage right [1 mark]
John following slowly behind and grumbling to himself [1 mark]	

Now try these
1. Children add stage directions to an extract from 'Cinderella'. Stage directions provided must be appropriate. They must include (Exit Ugly Sister) after her line: 'I must go and get myself ready for the ball' and (Enter Fairy Godmother) after Cinderella's line: 'I've got to clean the floor.'
2. Children choose another scene from 'Cinderella' or another traditional tale and write it as a playscript. Check that the script is correctly formatted according to the conventions outlined in **Get started**.

You may wish to use the activities and photocopiables in **Support and Embed** to give differentiated support with the writing tasks in **Now try these**.

Support, embed & challenge

Support
Unit 4 Resource 1: Stage directions provides a photocopiable version of question 1. For question 2: ask the children to highlight the dialogue in Unit 4 Resource 2: The glass slipper before working in pairs to create the playscript.

Embed
Once the children have completed question 1, ask them to use the text on Unit 4 Resource 2: The glass slipper or a scene from another fairy tale to create their playscript.

Challenge
Ask the children to choose a short story and rewrite it as a playscript. They could prepare the script for performance if time allows.

Homework / Additional activities

An argument
Ask the children to write a short scene in which two characters are arguing over something. Remind them to add stage directions so that the actors know how to say the words and what to do. Children might like to direct other pairs of children in a performance of their playscript, checking that the dialogue works well and that the stage directions are appropriate. They can then revise their playscripts.

Collins Connect: Unit 4
Ask the children to complete Unit 4 (See Teach → Year 5 → Composition → Unit 4).

Unit 5: Different kinds of recount (1)

Overview

English curriculum objectives

Writing – composition

Year 5 children should be taught to plan their writing by:

- identifying the audience for and purpose of the writing, selecting the appropriate form and using other similar writing as models for their own
- noting and developing initial ideas, drawing on reading.

Year 5 children should be taught to draft and write by selecting appropriate grammar and vocabulary, understanding how such choices can change and enhance meaning.

Notes and guidance (non-statutory)

Children should understand, through being shown, the skills and processes essential for writing.

Building towards

Children will discuss audience and purpose and write two different types of recount about the same event, making clear the distinctions between the two.

Treasure house resources

- Composition Skills Pupil Book 5, Unit 5, pages 20–23
- Collins Connect Treasure House Year 5, Unit 5
- Photocopiable Unit 5, Resource 1: Letter to a friend, page 73
- Photocopiable Unit 5, Resource 2: Magazine article, page 74

Additional resources

- Copies of children's newspapers for children to browse and read
- Children's TV news-style programmes
- Examples of personal letters, possibly drawn from books the children have read

Introduction

Teaching overview

This unit focuses on writing reports or recounts. The unit includes a newspaper article and a letter, both describing a fictitious football game, to compare and contrast the writing skills involved and to provide a model for children's own writing. The unit compares the features of both texts: one being an impersonal observation of the account, largely focusing on the facts of the event, the other being a personal account as a participant in the event, addressing a specific reader and describing the thoughts and feelings of the writer. Children are asked to write a letter to a friend describing a school trip they have been on. They then write about the same event again, but this time they write it as an article for the school magazine.

Introduce the concept

View, with the class, examples of children's television news or current affairs programmes. Discuss the impersonal (neutral) style of the reports, and ask children what the producer has had to consider regarding his or her audience and purpose. Look also at children's newspapers and discuss how the journalist has answered the '5Ws': Who? What? Where? When? Why?

Move on to provide examples of personal recounts of specific events written in a different form, for example letters or diary entries. These are personal reports and it is useful to compare and contrast these with the impersonal style of a newspaper report. Explain to children that in this unit they will compare and contrast two reports of the same event and be asked to write their own.

Read the two reports in the Pupil Book and ask the children to help you compare and contrast the two texts.

Unit 5: Different kinds of recount (1)

Pupil practice

Pupil Book pages 20–23

Get started
Children answer questions in discussion with a partner about previous texts they have written.

For each text mentioned, children discuss their reasons for writing it and who they wrote it for. They consider how the purpose and audience of each text affected the contents and writing style. They discuss which texts were more formal and which included more personal things such as thoughts and feelings. They compare texts they have written for themselves to the texts they have written for anyone to read.

Try these
Children complete a table with the information required, comparing and contrasting features of the two text types. Award 1 mark for each correct answer.

Newspaper report	Letter
Written in the third person	Written in the first person
Written for anyone to read	Written for a specific person
Asks the reader a question	Thoughts and feelings described
Events in chronological order	Events in chronological order
Written in the past tense	Written in the past tense

Now try these
1. Children write an informal letter to a friend telling them about a recent school trip they have been on. They are reminded to use informal language. Letters should include the thoughts and feelings of the writer and take a personal perspective.
2. Children write about the same event, but this time write it as an article for the school magazine. Reports should be written in the third person (impersonal) and the past tense. The information should be organised into paragraphs and more formal language should be used. It should aim to be an objective account of the event.

You may wish to use the activities and photocopiables in **Support and Embed** to give differentiated support with the writing tasks in **Now try these**.

Support, embed & challenge

Support
Ask the children to use Unit 5 Resource 1: Letter to a friend to write an informal letter telling a friend about a recent school trip (see **Now try these** question 1). provides useful prompts. Next, support the children as they convert the information into a formal third person report.

Embed
Encourage these children to create contrasting reports of the same event, using obviously informal and formal styles. Provide them with the templates on Unit 5 Resource 1: Letter to a friend and Resource 2: Magazine article. (see **Now try these** question 2). Unit 5 Resource 2: Magazine article provides a prompt.

Challenge
Ask the children to write about the same event, this time as a short diary entry using the first person. They should aim to open up a whole new perspective on the event. This activity looks forward to work in Unit 6.

Homework / Additional activities

Write a dramatic report
Ask the children to rewrite a dramatic scene from the class book as a newspaper report. They should come up with a striking headline to grab the reader's attention.

Collins Connect: Unit 5
Ask the children to complete Unit 5 (See Teach → Year 5 → Composition → Unit 5).

Unit 6: Different kinds of recount (2)

Overview

English curriculum objectives

Writing – composition

Year 5 children should be taught to plan their writing by:

- identifying the audience for and purpose of the writing, selecting the appropriate form and using other similar writing as models for their own
- noting and developing initial ideas, drawing on reading.

Year 5 children should be taught to draft and write by:

- selecting appropriate grammar and vocabulary, understanding how such choices can change and enhance meaning
- using a wide range of devices to build cohesion within and across paragraphs.

Notes and guidance (non-statutory)

Children should understand, through being shown, the skills and processes essential for writing.

Building towards

Children will write two first-person recounts of the same event, one formal and one informal.

Treasure house resources

- Composition Skills Pupil Book 5, Unit 6, pages 24–27
- Collins Connect Treasure House Year 5, Unit 6
- Photocopiable Unit 6, Resource 1: Police report, page 75
- Photocopiable Unit 6, Resource 2: Diary entry, page 76

Additional resources

- A short diary entry and police report derived from the same traditional story or fairy tale

Introduction

Teaching overview

This unit focuses on different sorts of records and builds on work in the previous unit where children explored the contrast between two recounts. The unit includes two more kinds of possible recount describing the same fictional event – a diary entry and a police report – for children to compare and contrast, and to stimulate children's own writing. The unit compares the features of both texts, one being an observational account, relating only the facts of the event, the other being a personal account of the event, written for the eye of the writer only and describing private thoughts and feelings. Children are asked to write a witness statement as part of a police report and to write about the same event in their personal diary to compare and contrast the two forms of recount writing.

Introduce the concept

Share with the class two different texts recounting a well-known traditional story or fairy tale (for example, 'Goldilocks and the Three Bears'): one a formal, factual police report detailing a 'crime' and the other a dairy entry written by the main character describing his or her feelings. Discuss the similarities and differences between the two in terms of language, audience, point of view and so on, and record children's ideas in a simple table:

	Features of a police report	Features of a dairy
Language	Formal, precise, fact-based	Informal, feelings-based
Audience	Other members of the police; lawyers	The writer himself or herself
Point of view	First person	First person

Children should discuss why the two text types are approached differently.

Unit 6: Different kinds of recount (2)

Pupil practice

Pupil Book pages 24–27

Get started
Children answer questions in discussion with a partner about the writing of and keeping of diaries. They discuss their knowledge of police reports. They think of other types of reporting texts (for example, newspaper reports, letters, minutes taken in a meeting).

Try these
1. Ask the children to read the two texts in the Pupil Book then complete a table with the features of the two text types.

   [1 mark for each correct feature]

Police report	Diary
Date of events	Date of events
Description of events	Description of events
Time of events	Thoughts and feelings
Value of stolen item	Hopes and wishes
Diagram of location	

2. Children write a sentence describing the purpose of each text type:

   A diary is a record of events that helps the writer remember and clarify an event that has happened to them.

   A police report is an outline of the facts of the event so that other people such as police officers, lawyers and judges can understand what happened and make fair decisions based on those facts. [2 marks]

Now try these
1. Children write a police statement about the discovery of the egg. The form should be correctly completed with time, location and witness name correctly added. The statement of events should be in chronological order and include only the relevant facts, observations and details.

2. Children write a diary entry about the day's events. Diary entries should be written in the first person and include thoughts and feelings.

You may wish to use the activities and photocopiables in **Support and Embed** to give differentiated support with the writing tasks in **Now try these**.

Support, embed & challenge

Support
Ask the children to use Unit 6 Resource 1: Police report as a support in writing a police report about the discovery of the egg (see **Now try these**). Ask the children to role-play phoning a friend from another school and telling them about their day, capturing thoughts and feelings and an informal, first person style.

Embed
Once the children have completed their police report, ask them to write about the same event, but this time write it as a diary entry. They include their thoughts and feelings. Unit 6 Resource 2: Diary entry provides a prompt.

Challenge
Ask the children to take an appropriate traditional tale or fairy tale (different from the one used in **Introduce the concept**) and write a police report.

Homework / Additional activities

Keeping your diary
Ask the children to keep a diary for a week. They should write in it each evening and add their thoughts and feelings about the events of their day. You may wish to allow children to keep their diaries private or you could suggest that they write an imaginary diary for someone or something else such as their favourite TV cartoon character or the class pet.

Collins Connect: Unit 6
Ask the children to complete Unit 6 (See Teach → Year 5 → Composition → Unit 6).

Unit 7: Writing narrative poems

Overview

English curriculum objectives

Reading – comprehension

Year 5 children should:
- learn a wider range of poetry by heart
- prepare poems to read aloud and to perform, showing understanding through intonation, tone and volume so that the meaning is clear to an audience.

Writing – composition

Year 5 children should be taught to plan their writing by:
- selecting the appropriate form and using other similar writing as models for their own
- noting and developing initial ideas, drawing on reading
- in writing narratives, considering how authors have developed characters and settings in what children have read.

Year 5 children should be taught to draft and write by:
- selecting appropriate grammar and vocabulary, understanding how such choices can change and enhance meaning
- in narratives, describing settings, characters and atmosphere and integrating dialogue to convey character and advance the action.

Notes and guidance (non-statutory)

Children should understand, through being shown, the skills and processes essential for writing.

Building towards

Children will plan and write their own narrative poem.

Treasure house resources

- Composition Skills Pupil Book 5, Unit 7, pages 28–31
- Collins Connect Treasure House Year 5, Unit 7
- Photocopiable Unit 7, Resource 1: Planning my narrative poem, page 77
- Photocopiable Unit 7, Resource 2: Writing my narrative poem, page 78

Additional resources

- A selection of narrative poems, including 'Flannan Isle' by Wilfrid Gibson and 'The Listeners' by Walter de la Mare
- A recorded reading of a narrative poem (optional)

Introduction

Teaching overview

This unit focuses on narrative poetry. Narrative poetry is a form of poetry that tells a story, often through the voice of a narrator. The entire story is usually written in metered verse (syllabic pattern). Narrative poems do not have to follow rhythmic patterns, but are often found written in rhyming couplets – *aabb*. Narrative poems include epics and ballads.

This unit includes a narrative poem, 'Kenneth' by Wendy Cope, as an example of this poetic form. It looks at its key features: narrators, characters, plot and settings, and considers other features common to narrative poetry such as rhyme scheme (rhyming couplets) and syllabic pattern (the number of syllables in a line). The unit gives a definition of narrative poetry. Children are asked to plan and write their own narrative poem including the features noted in the exemplar poem.

Wendy Cope (born 1945) is one of the UK's best-known contemporary poets, writing poetry for both adults and children that quite often has a wryly humorous flavour.

Introduce the concept

Ask children if they have ever read any narrative poetry before. The term 'narrative' may need clarifying. A narrative poem is a poem that tells a story. Read 'Kenneth' to the children, bringing out the drama. Share recordings of other narrative poems with the children.

Ask children to share what they notice about the features of this poetic form. Remind children of any work already carried out on plot structure and emphasise that narrative poetry always has a storyline. Narrative poems also sometimes contain a moral (as does the poem in the extract). You may wish to encourage the class to create storyboards of narrative poems, emphasising and exploring the plot, settings and characters through illustration.

Finally, remind children of the different rhyme patterns they have met before and used in their own poems. You may want to discuss syllabic patterns as well.

Unit 7: Writing narrative poems

Pupil practice

Pupil Book pages 28–31

Get started

1. Children answer questions in discussion with a partner about the meaning of the term 'narrative' and their experience of narrative poetry. They check their definitions using a dictionary (a narrative is a story) and discuss any narrative poems (a poem that tells a story) they know.

Try these

Children complete a list of the features of narrative poetry.

Answers

A narrative poem:
- tells a story with character and setting
- has beginning, middle and end
- sometimes has a moral
- often has a narrator who tells the story
- usually has a rhyme scheme – often *aabb*
- is usually quite long!

[1 mark for each feature given]

1. Children write two or three sentences saying why they think poems are a good way to tell a story. They may mention: the stanzas provide an effective structure (like paragraphs in prose stories); the rhyme scheme and syllabic pattern give the story a rhythm; the use of vivid language, including simile and metaphor.

Now try these

1. Children plan their idea for a narrative poem. The plan should include details of a setting, character, basic storyline, moral and choice of rhyme scheme.
2. Children write their narrative poem using their planning grid. They include all the features planned previously.

You may wish to use the activities and photocopiables in **Support and Embed** to give differentiated support with the writing projects in **Now try these**.

Support, embed & challenge

Support

Ask the children to plan the storyline, characters and setting for their own narrative poem. Unit 7 Resource 1: Planning my narrative poem supports this by providing a planning grid. Ensure that they have planned a relatively short and straightforward story to give them the best chance of turning it into a poem. Ask them to write their poem, attempting some rhyme.

Embed

Ask the children to write their narrative poem using the previously completed planning grid. Unit 7 Resource 2: Writing my narrative poem supports this. Once they've finished a first draft, challenge them to improve the rhythm and rhyme, asking a partner for suggestions.

Challenge

Ask the children to research other narrative poems, such as 'Flannan Isle' by Wilfrid Gibson or 'The Listeners' by Walter de la Mare. They should prepare a summary of the plot and plan their own mystery narrative poem.

Homework / Additional activities

A Cautionary Tale

Ask the children to research the Anglo-French poet and writer Hilaire Belloc (1870–1953) and choose one of his 'Cautionary Tales' to bring to school to read to the class.

Collins Connect: Unit 7

Ask the children to complete Unit 7 (See Teach → Year 5 → Composition → Unit 7).

Review unit 1

Pupil Book pages 32–33

These tasks provide the children with the opportunity to apply and demonstrate the skills they have learned.

Explain to the children that they now have an opportunity to show their skills independently. Read through the task with the children and make sure they have understood what to do.

A. Writing a diary entry

Look for evidence of children's developing understanding of and writing of diaries, as a personal kind of recount. Significant features to look out for include:

- first person
- past tense
- inclusion of the writer's hopes, wishes, thoughts and feelings.

B. Continuing a story

Look for evidence of children's developing understanding of and writing of narrative, especially how a plot might continue. Significant features to look out for include:

- the sequential nature of the additional episode
- inclusion of dialogue to move the action on
- use of past tense
- written in the relevant person (according to the point of view used in the original text).

C. Narrative poems

Look for evidence of children's developing understanding of narrative poetry. Significant features to look out for include:

- a storyline
- a strong rhyming scheme, such as *aabb*
- characters
- setting
- a moral (not essential), stated at the close.

Unit 8: Using linking words and phrases

Overview

English curriculum objectives

Writing – composition

Year 5 children should be taught to plan their writing by:

- identifying the audience for and purpose of the writing, selecting the appropriate form and using other similar writing as models for their own
- noting and developing initial ideas, drawing on reading.

Year 5 children should be taught to draft and write by:

- selecting appropriate grammar and vocabulary, understanding how such choices can change and enhance meaning
- using a wide range of devices to build cohesion within and across paragraphs
- linking ideas across paragraphs using adverbials of time (for example, later), place (for example, nearby) and number (for example, secondly).

Year 5 children should be taught to evaluate and edit by:

- assessing the effectiveness of their own and others' writing
- proposing changes to vocabulary, to enhance effects and clarify meaning.

Notes and guidance (non-statutory)

Children should understand, through being shown, the skills and processes essential for writing.

Building towards

Children will compose their own sentences using conjunctions (linking words and phrases).

Treasure house resources

- Composition Skills Pupil Book 5, Unit 8, pages 34–36
- Collins Connect Treasure House Year 5, Unit 8
- Photocopiable Unit 8, Resource 1: Adding linking words and phrases, page 79
- Photocopiable Unit 8, Resource 2: My sentences, page 80

Additional resources

- Copies of non-fiction texts, possibly drawn from the class topic or theme.

Introduction

Teaching overview

This unit focuses on using conjunctions (linking words and phrases) and includes a short explanation text to demonstrate the use of some of the relevant words and phrases. The unit includes an explanation of why it is important to use such joining words and phrases, and suggests some of the different functions they serve. Children are given the opportunity to practise using these words and phrases in sentences of their own, possibly related to the class topic.

Introduce the concept

Before you start the unit, it may be useful to remind children of the term 'conjunction' – a word or phrase that links phrases, sentences or paragraphs. Suggest that there are specific linking words and phrases relevant to non-fiction and, in particular, explanation text. Provide a selection of non-fiction texts for the children to use to search for different linking words, or source some grammar games and activities on conjunctions and linking phrases (adverbials). These will provide much-needed practice for children in selecting and using the right conjunction for the right task, and will go a long way towards clarifying for children what's required of them. For further practice, you may wish to provide children with extracts of texts where the linking words and phrases have been removed so they can add them back in. Some children will complete exercises like this independently while others will need additional support.

Pupil practice

Pupil Book pages 34–36

Get started

Children read the extract then work with a partner to define and then list a range of conjunctions.

Suggested answers

A conjunction is a word that connects words with words, phrases with phrases or clauses with clauses. Conjunctions link ideas within and across paragraphs. Children look back through their own writing and find examples of conjunctions. They compile a list of conjunctions they have used before.

Unit 8: Using linking words and phrases

Try these

Children complete a table adding words and phrases from the extract alongside their function. [1 mark for each correct example included in the correct row]

Answers

Function	Words and phrases from the extract
to add ideas or information	and, also, furthermore
to contrast two or more ideas	but
to show the result or indicate a consequence	as a result, therefore, so
to make a condition	if

Now try these

1. Children complete a table adding their own connecting words and phrases.

Possible answers

What is the function?	Connecting words and phrases
to add ideas or information	moreover, besides, in addition
to contrast two or more ideas	in contrast, nevertheless, on the other hand
to show the result or indicate a consequence	for this reason, consequently, thus
to make a condition	unless

2. Children write sentences using the connecting words and phrases they thought of previously.

You may wish to use the activities and photocopiables in **Support and Embed** to give differentiated support with the writing tasks in **Now try these**.

Support, embed & challenge

Support

Work as a group to research a list of words to complete the chart for **Now try these** question 1. As a group, verbally create sentences for the different words found. Ask the children to complete Unit 8 Resource 1: Adding linking words and phrases, which provides a simpler activity to replace **Now try these** question 2.

Embed

Ask the children to complete the table in **Now try these** question 1. Encourage them to use a thesaurus or the internet to extend their list of words and phrases. As they write their sentences for question 2, you may wish to provide them with Unit 8 Resource 2: My sentences to encourage them to be braver with their vocabulary choices.

Challenge

Ask these children to choose a topic that interests them where a process needs explaining. They compose the explanation using a variety of connecting words and phrases to link the ideas. They write and record this explanation.

Homework / Additional activities

Look, Cover, Write, Check

Ask the children to learn how to spell the following words using the Look, Cover, Write, Check process:
- consequently
- nevertheless
- moreover
- in addition
- besides

Collins Connect: Unit 8

Ask the children to complete Unit 8 (See Teach → Year 5 → Composition → Unit 8).

Unit 9: Character perspectives

Overview

English curriculum objectives

Writing – composition

Year 5 children should be taught to plan their writing by:
- selecting the appropriate form and using other similar writing as models for their own
- noting and developing initial ideas, drawing on reading.

Year 5 children should be taught to draft and write by:
- selecting appropriate grammar and vocabulary, understanding how such choices can change and enhance meaning
- in narratives, describing settings, characters and atmosphere and integrating dialogue to convey character and advance the action.

Notes and guidance (non-statutory)

Children should understand, through being shown, the skills and processes essential for writing.

Building towards

Children will write their own story where character perspective is developed.

Treasure house resources

- Composition Skills Pupil Book 5, Unit 9, pages 37–40
- Collins Connect Treasure House Year 5, Unit 9
- Photocopiable Unit 9, Resource 1: Goldilocks and Baby Bear, page 81
- Photocopiable Unit 9, Resource 2: A trip to the zoo, page 82

Additional resources

- One or two examples of traditional tales or fairy stories where the story is retold from the perspective of a different character, for children to discuss
- Clips from the film *Hoodwinked!* (2005), which tells the story 'Red Riding Hood' from four different character perspectives

Introduction

Teaching overview

This unit focuses on writing from a character's perspective. The unit uses an extract from *Underground to Canada* by the American writer Barbara Smucker (1915–2003) to demonstrate the writing skills involved and to provide a model for children's own writing. The unit defines character perspective and explores the perspectives of the characters in the extract. Children look for evidence of character perspective. They are given the opportunity to write a story from one of several character perspectives. They choose from the given titles, one of which is to retell a traditional tale from another character's point of view.

'Character perspective' differs from 'point of view' in that the latter usually refers to the 'person' used to tell a story (usually first or third person). For example, a story can be told in the third person but be told from a character's or several characters' perspective.

Introduce the concept

Begin by the lesson by reading one or two 'reworkings' of a traditional tale where it is told from a different character's point of view (for example, the wolf's rather than Red Riding Hood's). Or you could show clips from the film *Hoodwinked*, which shows the story from multiple perspectives. It may also be useful to discuss the perspectives of characters in fiction that children are already familiar with. Hot-seating provides a means of character analysis.

Asking children to defend well-known villainous characters is a particularly useful way to consider alternative perspectives and show bias in narratives. You might ask children to role-play the wolf in the story of 'Red Riding Hood' giving his defence in court.

Children need to know that changing perspective does not mean changing the facts of the story, only how those facts are experienced and interpreted. They should understand the difference, too, between perspective and point of view.

Pupil practice

Pupil Book pages 37–40

Get started

Children work with a partner to discuss perspective and point of view.

Answers

1. Character perspective is what a character, or group of characters, see, think and feel from their particular position in the story.

Unit 9: Character perspectives

2. A narrator is the person (or animal or thing) that tells the story.
3. A first person narrator is a character in the story, narrating in the first person. A third person narrator is not part of the story and narrates a character or characters' perspective.
4. First person narration can provide the thoughts and feelings of a character and conveys a clear version of events with a real sense of the reader seeing things through the character's eyes. However, it limits the possibility of viewing the story from different character perspectives and, as such, key information may be missing.
5. A third person omniscient narrator is a narrator who knows what all the characters are thinking and doing.

Try these
Children read the text, then complete a table showing the two main perspectives in the extract.

[1 mark for each correct point.]

	The slaves	The slave owners
What is their position in society (their social status)?	Very low – they are the property of other people.	High status – they own the property (slaves).
What do they hope for in the future? Do they have any plans?	Hope to stay on Hensens' plantation. They have families and the Hensens are 'soft' slave owners. They wish to be free.	They intend to sell the plantation and retire due to sickness, old age and lack of an heir. They hope for a comfortable retirement.
What are they afraid of?	The Hensens will sell them to cruel plantation owners. Their families will be broken up.	The future of their plantation. Their finances. That the slaves will rebel.

Now try these
1. Children think of a story with two viewpoints. They retell it from one character's perspective. The story should be a first-person account from the perspective of one of the characters.
2. Children tell the same story, this time from another character's perspective. The story should be another first-person account from the point of view of another character.

You may wish to use the activities and photocopiables in **Support and Embed** to give differentiated support with the writing tasks in **Now try these**.

Support, embed & challenge

Support
Ask the children to retell the story of 'Goldilocks and the Three Bears' from the perspective of first Goldilocks and then Baby Bear. Unit 9 Resource 1: Goldilocks and Baby Bear provides a planning template to help them.

Embed
Ask these children to use either 'The theft' or 'A trip to the zoo' for their writing project, challenging them to bring out some of the moral issues. Unit 9 Resource 2: A trip to the zoo provides support for the second of these stories.

Challenge
Ask the children to choose another of the choice of titles in **Now try these** and write a story from one of the characters' perspectives. They should write in the third person, but still try to show the story from their chosen character's perspective.

Homework / Additional activities

Writing arguments
Ask the children to write the story of an argument between brother and sister. Ask them to write two paragraphs about the argument – one from each perspective. They can use first or third person.

Collins Connect: Unit 9
Ask the children to complete Unit 9 (See Teach → Year 5 → Composition → Unit 9).

39

Unit 10: Dialogue

Overview

English curriculum objectives

Writing – composition

Year 5 children should be taught to plan their writing by:

- selecting the appropriate form and using other similar writing as models for their own
- noting and developing initial ideas, drawing on reading
- in writing narratives, considering how authors have developed characters and settings in what children have read, listened to or seen performed.

Year 5 children should be taught to draft and write by:

- selecting appropriate grammar and vocabulary, understanding how such choices can change and enhance meaning
- in narratives, describing characters and integrating dialogue to convey character and advance the action.

Vocabulary, grammar and punctuation (from Year 4)

[Children should be introduced to the] use of inverted commas and other punctuation to indicate direct speech.

Notes and guidance (non-statutory)

Children should understand, through being shown, the skills and processes essential for writing.

Building towards

Children will plan a short piece of dialogue that should develop the reader's understanding of the characters portrayed.

Treasure house resources

- Composition Skills Pupil Book 5, Unit 10, pages 41–44
- Collins Connect Treasure House Year 5, Unit 10
- Photocopiable Unit 10, Resource 1: Plan for a conversation in a shop, page 83
- Photocopiable Unit 10, Resource 2: Dialogue in a shop, page 84

Additional resources

- A selection of stories where dialogue is used effectively to portray character or move the action on, for children to browse and read
- Scenes from films, television programmes and comic strips that include dialogue for children to analyse and discuss (optional)

Introduction

Teaching overview

This unit focuses on using dialogue to develop characters. The unit includes an extract from *Jazeera in the Sun* by Lisa Bruce to illustrate the writing skills involved and to provide a model for children's writing. The unit looks at the various uses for dialogue (to show what people think and feel, show relationships, move the plot forward and impart information to the reader) and focuses on what the dialogue in the extract demonstrates about the characters. Children are given the opportunity to develop and write their own scene, integrating dialogue and description to develop their characters.

Introduce the concept

Ask children to share what they know about the uses of dialogue in narrative with each other Take feedback and summarise as above. At this point it would be useful to look at some examples of dialogue from classroom texts and classic novels. It may also be useful to provide scenes from films, television programmes and comic strips that include dialogue for children to analyse and discuss what purpose the dialogue serves.

Read the extract with the children. Ask them to locate places where plot, relationship and character are shown through dialogue.

Pupil practice

Pupil Book pages 41–44

Get started

Children work with a partner to answer questions about the use of dialogue in texts and the correct method of punctuation.

Answers

1–3. Children look back through their work to find examples of dialogue in narrative and discuss why it was used and whether the dialogue achieved what they were aiming for.

Unit 10: Dialogue

4. Children write a list of rules for correctly punctuated dialogue:
- Put speech marks at the start and the end of spoken words.
- Put a capital letter at the start of the speech.
- Start a new line for each new speaker.
- Add punctuation (full stops, question marks and exclamation marks) before the closing speech marks.

5. Dialogue can be used for showing what characters think or feel; showing relationships between characters; to move the plot forward; and to pass on information or explain things to the reader.

Try these
Children answer questions relating to the dialogue in the text.

Answers
1. The woman has a strong personality and is assertive and argumentative. [1 mark]
2. The girls do not speak at any point. [1 mark]
3. It stops the reader from getting to know the girls. [1 mark]
4. The woman buys the bangles from Ibrahim for 100 rupees (which confuses Jazeera). [1 mark]
5. We know that Uncle Salim is pleased because he says, "Very good." [1 mark]
6. Jazeera speaks softly because she is worried about what she has to say. [1 mark]
7. Uncle Salim is also explaining haggling to the reader. [1 mark]
8. It tells the reader that she is struggling to get to grips with Indian culture. [1 mark]
9. Uncle Salim says, "Shopping here is not like shopping in England, where everything has a fixed price on the label. In India, we argue about the price." [1 mark]
10. We learn this when Uncle Salim says, "I know that my shop is in good hands when I leave it with him…" [1 mark]

Now try these
1. Children write a summary of a conversation that could occur in a shop. They give brief descriptions of the characters. The conversation should feature two people in a shop. Summaries should include details of the plot and character descriptions of the two people who will hold the conversation.
2. Children write the dialogue in narrative form. The dialogue should feature the two people in the previous plot summary and reveal their personalities through the words they say and how they speak.

You may wish to use the activities and photocopiables in **Support and Embed** to give differentiated support with the writing tasks in **Now try these**.

Support, embed & challenge

Support
Ask the children, in pairs, to role-play three different conversations that could take place in a shop. Ask them to change partners between each role play. Encourage them to try out playing different characters, and take on different roles (shopper, shopkeeper). Ask them to choose two interesting characters and complete Unit 10 Resource 1: Plan for a conversation in a shop, before writing their conversation with support if needed.

Embed
Ask the children to write the dialogue for the shop scene. Encourage them to think about character, plot and atmosphere and think carefully about how they can capture this in the dialogue. Unit 10 Resource 2: Dialogue in a shop provides a template for their final dialogue.

Challenge
Give these children the title of a short story: 'That's mine!' and ask them to write the opening dialogue, remembering that one of the uses of dialogue is to move the action on and describe character.

Homework / Additional activities

An overheard conversation
Ask the children to write a short piece of dialogue, playscript style, based on something they have overheard at school or at home. There should be two or three people in the dialogue. The dialogue should show the characters of the people speaking.

Collins Connect: Unit 10
Ask the children to complete Unit 10 (See Teach → Year 5 → Composition → Unit 10).

Unit 11: Writing a persuasive letter

Overview

English curriculum objectives

Writing – composition

Year 5 children should be taught to plan their writing by:

- identifying the audience for and purpose of the writing, selecting the appropriate form and using other similar writing as models for their own
- noting and developing initial ideas, drawing on reading.

Year 5 children should be taught to draft and write by:

- selecting appropriate grammar and vocabulary, understanding how such choices can change and enhance meaning
- using a wide range of devices to build cohesion within and across paragraphs.

Year 5 children should be taught to evaluate and edit by assessing the effectiveness of their own and others' writing.

Notes and guidance (non-statutory)

Children should understand, through being shown, the skills and processes essential for writing.

Building towards

Children will write their own persuasive letter.

Treasure house resources

- Composition Skills Pupil Book 5, Unit 11, pages 45–47
- Collins Connect Treasure House Year 5, Unit 11
- Photocopiable Unit 11, Resource 1: Planning my persuasive letter, page 85
- Photocopiable Unit 11, Resource 2: My persuasive letter, page 86

Additional resources

- Copies of example persuasive letters, perhaps complaint letters
- Examples of formal letters, possibly sent to local newspapers about a specific local issue

Introduction

Teaching overview

This unit focuses on writing a persuasive letter. It includes an example of a fictitious letter that aims to persuade the local parliamentary representative (MP) to support the re-employment of the crossing patrol person/crossing guard. This example seeks to demonstrate the writing skills involved and to provide a model for children's writing. The unit looks at how to order and structure information, and how to link supporting points with connecting words and phrases. Children are given the opportunity to plan and write their own persuasive letter in support of a cause of their choice.

The unit also reviews the conventions of formal letter writing (see Year 4, Unit 15), including the correct greetings and sign-off for such letters.

Introduce the concept

Ask children to share their knowledge of formal letter writing with their partner and take feedback. Ask: 'Do you remember how to set out a letter?' Tell the class that this unit of work relates to writing a formal persuasive letter and that there are a few different features to consider. At this point it may be useful to provide examples of formal letters. Photocopy some and distribute them to the class. Children should work in pairs to read out the letters as in a role-play situation, using expression and intonation. Ask them what they notice about the structure of the information, the language used and the greeting and sign-off.

To start children expressing their own opinions, you may wish to discuss children's views on global, national, and/or local issues.

Unit 11: Writing a persuasive letter

Pupil practice

Pupil Book pages 45–47

Get started

Children work with a partner discussing the sending and receiving of persuasive letters, the conventions of letter writing and the reasons for writing persuasive letters.

Answers

1. Children discuss letters/emails they have written/received in the past.

2. The conventions of formal letter writing:
   - sender's address in the top right-hand corner
   - date beneath the sender's address
   - recipient's address on the left-hand side, after the line with the date on
   - greeting – do you know the person's name?
   - use of paragraphs to structure what you want to say
   - the correct sign-off ('Yours faithfully' to match 'Dear Sir/Madam'; 'Yours sincerely' if the letter is to a named person) and your name/signature.

3. Children list reasons for writing a persuasive letter/email, for example to persuade people to give to a charity or to persuade a government to take action on an issue.

Try these

Children read the extract and answer specific questions about the formal letter.

Answers

1. The letter aims to persuade Mrs Hoyle. [1 mark]

2. Mrs Hoyle is the local Member of Parliament so she is responsible for making decisions about this issue. [1 mark]

3. The aim is to persuade Mrs Hoyle to support the re-employment of the crossing patrol person. [1 mark]

4. The writer provides the results of a survey that shows many children do use the crossing. The writer also argues that, even if fewer children used the crossing, guaranteeing their safety would still be very important. [1 mark]

5. Paragraph 1: They are writing to express concerns about road safety outside the school.

Paragraph 2: They understand that children will no longer be assisted in crossing the road.

Paragraph 3: The reason from the council is that the crossing isn't used enough.

Paragraph 4: The results of the survey show that it is used by many children.

Paragraph 5: Even if fewer children used the crossing, guaranteeing their safety would still be very important.

Paragraph 6: To conclude, they ask the MP to ask the council to reconsider its decision. [1 mark per paragraph]

6. The language is formal and polite. [1 mark]

7. 'First', 'Second', On the basis of this evidence'. [1 mark]

8. Things to consider when writing a persuasive letter:
   - Who do you want to persuade and therefore to whom should you write?
   - What do you want to persuade the person about?
   - What facts and evidence do you have to support your argument?

How should the argument be structured?
[1 mark per correct sentence]

Now try these

1. Children plan a persuasive letter about their chosen issue. The letter should be planned using the correct layout and it should be clear that the structure presents an organised argument.

2. Children write a persuasive letter about their chosen issue. Their letter should adhere to the letter-writing conventions detailed in the unit. There should be a well-structured argument, a clear purpose and the use of formal language.

You may wish to use the activities and photocopiables in **Support and Embed** to give differentiated support with the writing tasks in **Now try these**.

Unit 11: Writing a persuasive letter

Support, embed & challenge

Support
In a group, discuss the different issues that the children want to write about. Support each child as they articulate their point of view. Provide further arguments and facts that each child might want to use. Ask them plan using Unit 11 Resource 1: Planning my persuasive letter. Remind them to use the letter in the extract as a model as they write their letter.

Embed
Ask the children to take turns in pairs to practise giving their verbal arguments in favour of their chosen cause. Tell the listening child to ask questions about the cause to encourage their partner to think more clearly about their arguments. Ask the children to plan their letter using the table in **Now try these** question 1 and then write their final letter on Unit 11 Resource 2: My persuasive letter. They should use their previous planning, write in full sentences and use formal language.

Challenge
Ask the children to consider an issue in their locality that they feel strongly about and write to their local newspaper or to their parliamentary representative. They should follow the conventions of formal letter writing and await a reply or see whether their letter is published!

Homework / Additional activities

Write to the Prime Minister
Ask the class to decide on an important national issue that concerns them. Ask the children to research the issue and then write some notes about what could be included in a letter to the Prime Minister/First Minister to persuade him or her to adopt their point of view. The children feed back their ideas to the class and a class letter is written.

Collins Connect: Unit 11
Ask the children to complete Unit 11 (See Teach → Year 5 → Composition → Unit 11).

Unit 12: Writing factual reports and opinion pieces

Overview

English curriculum objectives

Writing – composition

Year 5 children should be taught plan their writing by:

- identifying the audience for and purpose of the writing, selecting the appropriate form and using other similar writing as models for their own
- noting and developing initial ideas, drawing on reading.

Year 5 children should be taught to draft and write by:

- selecting appropriate grammar and vocabulary, understanding how such choices can change and enhance meaning
- using a wide range of devices to build cohesion within and across paragraphs.

Year 5 children should be taught to evaluate and edit by assessing the effectiveness of their own and others' writing.

Notes and guidance (non-statutory)

Children should understand, through being shown, the skills and processes essential for writing.

Building towards

Children will write a newspaper report and an editorial about a fictitious event.

Treasure house resources

- Composition Skills Pupil Book 5, Unit 12, pages 48–51
- Collins Connect Treasure House Year 5, Unit 12
- Photocopiable Unit 12, Resource 1: My newspaper report, page 87
- Photocopiable Unit 12, Resource 2: My newspaper editorial, page 88

Additional resources

- Children's newspapers or a selection of appropriate articles from daily papers – print-based or online
- School magazine articles or write-ups of past school events
- Copies of appropriate editorials from newspapers

Introduction

Teaching overview

This unit focuses on the presentation of facts and opinions in texts. The unit uses two example newspaper articles to exemplify the writing skills involved and to provide a model for children's writing. The unit provides definitions of 'fact' and 'opinion' and focuses on differentiating between the two. Children are given the opportunity to write their own newspaper reports, one reporting the facts of a fictional event, and one editorial article providing a personal response to the same events (an opinion piece).

Introduce the concept

It may be useful before starting to provide children with examples of facts and opinions to familiarise them with the difference. You might like to follow this up by providing children with a list of sentences, some of which are factual and some opinions, and asking them to decide which is which. Statements of opinion sometimes include indicative words and phrases such as 'In my opinion ...', 'I believe ...' and 'I would argue that ...'.

Ask the children to look through a selection of school newsletters and children's newspapers and locate facts and opinions.

Pupil practice

Pupil Book pages 48–51

Get started

Children work with a partner to discuss the difference between fact and opinion.

Answers

1. A fact is a piece of information that cannot be argued against.
2. Children think of some examples of facts.
3. An opinion is a personal view or belief that cannot be proved.
4. Children think of some examples of opinions.
5. An editorial is a type of news article in which the writer expresses their opinion or the opinion of the newspaper.

Try these

1. Ask the children to read the extract and then find examples of facts and opinions from the extracts.

    [1 mark for each example in the correct column]

45

Unit 12: Writing factual reports and opinion pieces

Suggested answers

Facts	Opinions
The protestors chose to protest on a Thursday evening.	beautiful countryside
At about 9:30 a spokesperson came out.	"This is good news" (a quoted opinion)
Mr Green organised the protest.	The wind farm will be unsightly and noisy.
Hordington is a small market town.	We cannot expect other people in other places will solve the problem.
People gathered in the main car park and marched to the Town Hall carrying banners and chanting, "No wind farm!"	This is not good enough.
	People who live in Hordington and the surrounding areas do not want their countryside spoilt by a wind farm.

2. Children state in which text they found the most opinions and in which the most facts. They should find more facts in the news report, though some opinions may be found given in quotes or clearly marked as being the opinion of the participants (for example, 'people ... are worried that'). The editorial will have most opinions, though once again there will also be some facts mentioned to support the opinions.

Now try these

1. Children write a report of an event as it would have appeared in the local newspaper. Their report should describe the demonstration and may include the opinions of the protesters. It will be written in the third person.

2. Children write an editorial about an event, explaining their opinions about the issue and the demonstration. Their editorial will express the opinions of the writer as well as reporting on the facts. It will be written in the first person.

You may wish to use the activities and photocopiables in **Support and Embed** to give differentiated support with tthe writing activities in **Now try these**.

Support, embed & challenge

Support
These children focus on **Now try these** question 1. Ask them to make up an event, noting down details, including one quotation. Discuss their ideas with them, helping them to locate fact and opinion in their planning before they write. Unit 12 Resource 1: My newspaper report provides a newspaper template for the children to write on.

Embed
Once these children have completed question 1, recap on the difference between a newspaper report and an editorial. Explain that in question 2, they should explain their opinion – summarising this in their headline – as well as reporting events. Unit 12 Resource 2: My newspaper editorial provides an editorial template for them to write on.

Challenge
Ask the children to consider an issue they feel strongly about. They write an article about this issue, expressing their opinions.

Homework / Additional activities

Your editorial
Ask the children to write an editorial about a news issue of the day. They should be prepared to share the piece orally with the class, giving thought to their intonation and presentation.

Collins Connect: Unit 12
Ask the children to complete Unit 12 (See Teach → Year 5 → Composition → Unit 12).

Unit 13: Writing for an audience

Overview

English curriculum objectives

Writing – composition

Year 5 children should be taught to plan their writing by:

- identifying the audience and purpose of the writing, selecting the appropriate form and using other similar writing as models for their own
- noting and developing initial ideas, drawing on reading.

Year 5 children should be taught to draft and write by:

- selecting appropriate grammar and vocabulary, understanding how such choices can change and enhance meaning
- in narratives, describing settings, characters and atmosphere and integrating dialogue to convey character and advance the action.

Notes and guidance (non-statutory)

Children should understand, through being shown, the skills and processes essential for writing.

Building towards

Children will write two versions of a traditional tale, each with a specific audience (readership) in mind.

Treasure house resources

- Composition Skills Pupil Book 5, Unit 13, pages 52–55
- Collins Connect Treasure House Year 5, Unit 13
- Photocopiable Unit 13, Resource 1: A tale for older children, page 89
- Photocopiable Unit 13, Resource 2: A tale for younger children, page 90

Additional resources

- Clips from films of traditional tales
- Selection of traditional tales or fairy stories written for a range of readerships (Reception, Key Stage 1, Key Stage 2) for children to browse and read
- Picture books for older children for children to investigate (see Challenge)

Introduction

Teaching overview

This unit focuses on writing for different audiences. The unit includes two versions of the same story, written for different aged readerships, to exemplify the writing skills involved and to provide a model for children's own writing. The unit looks at what makes each version of the story suitable for its intended audience. Children are given the opportunity to write their own story for older children and then adapt it to be read by younger children.

Introduce the concept

Before starting it may be useful to show children examples of stories where more than one version has been written for different audiences. View clips from films of traditional tales aimed at both younger and older children and discuss what age the film is aimed at and what makes them think that.

Non-fiction texts can also be used for comparison as the same facts are often presented differently according to the age or expected level of prior knowledge of the readership. Some of the Collins Big Cat series books would provide excellent examples if earlier and later reading bands are chosen. Children could investigate the language used, the number and kind of illustrations, the use of dialogue, and the sentence construction as they consider the readership.

Unit 13: Writing for an audience

Pupil practice

Pupil Book pages 52–55

Get started
Children think of a book they read when they were younger and share this with a partner. They should discuss issues such as its title, what it was about, what they liked about it and what illustrations it had.

Try these
Children answer questions about the two text extracts.

Answers
1. Both use language, both are illustrated and both tell the same story. [1 mark]
2. The version for older children uses paragraphs. [1 mark]
3. The version for older children uses different words for the word 'said'. [1 mark]
4. The version for younger children uses mostly pictures to tell the story. [1 mark]
5. The version for older children includes dialogue. [1 mark]
6. Pictures help younger children to understand what the words mean. [1 mark]
7. Pictures have the advantage that they can communicate things anyone can understand regardless of language or reading ability. [1 mark]
8. Words have the advantage that they describe things more precisely and often in more detail than pictures. [1 mark]

Now try these
1. Children retell a traditional tale using the language and other features similar to those used in the first extract.
2. Children rewrite the traditional tale, adapting it for younger readers. Their rewrite should show evidence that they have considered how to adapt the story for young readers, both in terms of what they need to add and what should be removed or changed. They should include pictures to help young readers understand the story.

You may wish to use the activities and photocopiables in **Support and Embed** to give differentiated support with the writing tasks in **Now try these**.

Support, embed & challenge

Support
Ask the children to focus on **Now try these** question 1. Tell them to use the style of the first extract in the Pupil Book as a model for retelling another traditional tale (provide a selection to choose from). Unit 13 Resource 1: A tale for older children provides a checklist and a space for writing.

Embed
After completing question 1, ask these children to move on to complete question 2. The checklist in Unit 13 Resource 2: A tale for younger children supports them with this.

Challenge
Ask the children to investigate wordless picture books for older children. When an example or two have been found, the children should write a few sentences explaining why the book is suitable for an older readership even though there is no written language present.

Homework / Additional activities

Storyboarding for younger children
Ask the children to choose a storybook and then take a chapter or an episode and draw it as a wordless storyboard so that younger children can understand and enjoy it. They might like to try out their picture books on younger children in their school, and assess whether the story is clear and enjoyable for its target audience.

Collins Connect: Unit 13
Ask the children to complete Unit 13 (See Teach → Year 5 → Composition → Unit 13).

Unit 14: Describing settings

Overview

English curriculum objectives

Writing – composition

Year 5 children should be taught to plan their writing by:

- selecting the appropriate form and using other similar writing as models for their own
- noting and developing initial ideas, drawing on reading
- in writing narratives, considering how authors have developed characters.

Year 5 children should be taught to draft and write by:

- selecting appropriate grammar and vocabulary, understanding how such choices can change and enhance meaning
- in narratives, describing settings, characters and atmosphere and integrating dialogue to convey character and advance the action.

Notes and guidance (non-statutory)

Children should understand, through being shown, the skills and processes essential for writing.

Building towards

The children will write their own descriptive paragraph.

Treasure house resources

- Composition Skills Pupil Book 5, Unit 14, pages 56–58
- Collins Connect Treasure House Year 5, Unit 14
- Photocopiable Unit 14, Resource 1: Planning the description, page 91
- Photocopiable Unit 14, Resource 2: My descriptive paragraph, page 92

Additional resources

- Clips from a range of children's film openings – openings in films are often 'establishing' shots, establishing the setting of the film
- A selection of story settings, from short stories or novels, where descriptive language has been used to paint a picture of the setting in the reader's eye

Introduction

Teaching overview

This unit focuses on describing settings and provides three setting descriptions to demonstrate the writing skills involved and to provide a model for children's own writing. The unit analyses the various descriptive techniques used in each setting description. Children are given the opportunity to attempt some of the descriptive techniques exemplified and then to write their own setting description.

Introduce the concept

It may be useful before starting to look at a range of example settings. Openings in films are often 'establishing' shots, establishing the setting of the film. Ask children to note what the camera (as a kind of 'narrator') is showing the viewer. Pause as the camera moves to different shots and ask children to give descriptive words, noun phrases, similes and so on to describe what they see. The same could be done with pictures or images on an interactive whiteboard. Examples drawn from books could then be used for analysis by asking children to highlight descriptive language and language referring to the senses.

Pupil practice

Pupil Book pages 56–58

Get started

Children complete the tasks with a partner.

Answers

1. They make lists of what they can see, hear, smell and feel around the classroom.
2. They take three coloured pencils and underline the adjectives, verbs and nouns in their lists in different colours.
3. They consider their choice of vocabulary and make improvements if they can.

Try these

1. Children read the text and complete a table, adding information from the extracts about sensory description.

Children may list some of the following.

[1 mark for each piece of sensory description added into the correct column]

Unit 14: Describing settings

	Sights	Sounds	Smells
The forest	black night sky the trees swaying	screech of an owl Tom's pounding heart	the scent of decaying leaves
The kitchen	tiny, steamy kitchen people everywhere pots and pans everywhere table mountain of food Dad Billy (tripping over a stool)	talking bubbling, rattling pots	delicious smell of food
The cinema	flickering bluish light	everything becomes quiet rustling of wrapping paper people fumbling quietly in their bags	aroma of warm popcorn

Children find one example from each of the following lists.

2. *Alliteration:* blinding blackness; face like fingers; crowded and chaotic; pots and pans [1 mark]
3. *Similes:* branches that clutch like fingers; trees that whisper like conspirators; a kitchen as crowded and as chaotic as a funfair [1 mark]
4. *Personification:* a treacherous screech; a sky that yawns; branches that are fingers; trees that conspire; a table that groans [1 mark]
5. *Hyperbole:* pots and pans piled toweringly high; a mountain of food; a smile that's warmer than sunshine [1 mark]

Now try these

1. Children choose a setting from a given list and plan their descriptive piece using the planning grid provided. Children's planning should include details of sights, sounds and smells; ideas for alliteration; a simile; a metaphor; personification and hyperbole.
2. Using their planning, children write their own descriptive piece including the features listed.

You may wish to use the activities and photocopiables in **Support and Embed** to give differentiated support with the writing tasks in **Now try these**.

Support, embed & challenge

Support
Ask the children to choose a setting from a given list and plan their descriptive piece using the planning grid provided in Unit 14 Resource 1: Planning the description. Ask the children to draw a picture of their setting and write extensive descriptive labels for it as well as a caption.

Embed
Ask the children to use their planning to write their own descriptive paragraph. The checklist in Unit 14 Resource 2: My descriptive paragraph supports them with this.

Challenge
Ask children to take a walk in the school grounds and to choose somewhere to sit. Ask them to write a descriptive paragraph of the school grounds for inclusion in the school magazine or prospectus.

Homework / Additional activities

Where I want to be
Ask the children to draw a picture of a setting where they would like to be. Add descriptive words and phrases next to the picture to make everything as vivid as possible.

Collins Connect: Unit 14
Ask the children to complete Unit 14 (See Teach → Year 5 → Composition → Unit 14).

Review unit 2

Pupil Book pages 59–60

These tasks provide the children with the opportunity to apply and demonstrate the skills they have learned.

Explain to the children that they now have an opportunity to show their skills independently. Read through the task with the children and make sure they have understood what to do.

A. Dialogue

Look for evidence of children's developing understanding of and writing of dialogue. Significant features to look out for include:

- dialogue to show what characters are thinking or feeling
- dialogue to show relationships between the characters
- dialogue to move the plot forward
- dialogue to pass on information or explain things to the reader.

Also check for the correct presentation of dialogue in a story, although this is of secondary concern here.

B. Writing a persuasive letter

Look for evidence of children's developing understanding of and writing of a persuasive letter. Significant features to look out for include:

- adherence to the letter-writing conventions
- a well-structured argument using paragraphs
- a clear purpose
- the use of formal language.

C. Writing a newspaper report and editorial

Look for evidence of children's developing understanding of the difference between reporting facts and opinions. Significant features to look out for include:

Report:

- third person
- mainly facts, though the inclusion of the reported opinions of participants is possible.

Editorial:

- first person
- opinions of the writer as well as reporting on the facts.

Unit 15: Conveying atmosphere

Overview

English curriculum objectives

Writing – composition

Year 5 children should be taught to plan their writing by:
- identifying the audience for and purpose of the writing, selecting the appropriate form and using other similar writing as models for their own
- noting and developing initial ideas, drawing on reading
- in writing narratives, considering how authors have developed characters.

Year 5 children should be taught to draft and write by:
- selecting appropriate grammar and vocabulary, understanding how such choices can change and enhance meaning
- in narratives, describing settings, characters and atmosphere and integrating dialogue to convey character and advance the action.

Notes and guidance (non-statutory)

Children should understand, through being shown, the skills and processes essential for writing.

Building towards

Children will plan and then write two atmospheric and contrasting paragraphs of their own.

Treasure house resources

- Composition Skills Pupil Book 5, Unit 15, pages 61–64
- Collins Connect Treasure House Year 5, Unit 15
- Photocopiable Unit 15, Resource 1: Planning the paragraph, page 93
- Photocopiable Unit 15, Resource 2: Conveying atmosphere, page 94

Additional resources

- Images of paintings with different atmospheric settings, for example, a sunny river landscape, a night-time sky or a snowy scene, for children to describe and contrast
- A selection of novels with atmospheric settings for children to browse and read

Introduction

Teaching overview

This unit focuses on conveying atmosphere. The unit uses two contrasting setting descriptions to demonstrate the writing skills involved and to provide models for children's own writing. The unit analyses the various descriptive techniques used in each setting description. Children are given the opportunity to attempt some of the descriptive techniques exemplified and then to write their own contrasting setting descriptions.

Introduce the concept

Prior to beginning this unit, ask children to describe a series of paintings with differing but strong moods. Ask them to comment particularly on how each painter has conveyed mood or atmosphere. You might, for example, contrast an Impressionist/Post-impressionist painting of a sunny river landscape (for example, one of Claude Monet's paintings at Argenteuil) with another of a night-time scene (for example, Vincent van Gogh's *Starry Night*) or with a snowy scene (for example, Alfred Sisley's *Snow at Louveciennes*). You could try asking for specific types of description such as noun phrases, personification, similes or metaphors – this builds on work in Unit 14. Share the settings in a range of novels. Ask them to discuss these with a partner.

Pupil practice

Pupil Book pages 61–64

Get started

Children discuss the questions and complete the tasks with a partner. They describe the school playground by day and by night. They compare the two descriptions considering how the atmosphere changes. Children describe their happiest memories: where they were and what they remember about their surroundings. Children talk about a scary, spooky or creepy story or film they have read or seen, discussing the setting and how that creepy atmosphere was created.

Try these

Children complete a table, listing features of the descriptions. Children do not need to find all of these.

[1 mark for each descriptive feature]

Unit 15: Conveying atmosphere

	The waiting room	The wedding
Sights	rain against window; swinging doors; heads turning	sunshine, open doors, people on the lawn, children, a bride, familiar faces, the bride's husband, father and brother
Sounds	tapping rain; the odd cough; people breathing; footsteps clicking, rhythmic swish and thud of doors	People chatting and laughing, children playing and calling, music, the sound of deep voices, rhythms, men laughing and joking
Smells	bleach, sickness	the drifting scent of roses
Adjectives	impatient, silent, odd, tangible, touchable, rhythmic	full, open, lazy, bronzed, familiar, deep
Verbs	tapped, consenting, dared, speak, stop, thinking, cough, hacked, swung, turned, held, released, hissing, clicked, followed, accompanied, went	shone, wanted, flung, letting, drifting, strewn, chatting, laughing, playing, calling, walked, blowing, greeted, congratulated, danced, mingled, see, laughing, joking
Adverbs	insistently, mutually, expectantly	brightly, gently
Emotions	impatience, tension, disappointment, relief	excitement

Now try these

1. Children choose a setting to describe. They use the planning grid provided to guide them. Their notes should show a good contrast between the settings.

2. Using their planning, children write two atmospheric paragraphs. There should be a good contrast between the settings. The paragraphs should feature expanded noun phrases, interesting and powerful verbs, and expressive vocabulary.

You may wish to use the activities and photocopiables in **Support and Embed** to give differentiated support with the writing projects in **Now try these**.

Support, embed & challenge

Support
Ask the children to choose a setting to describe both by day and night. Share ideas for each setting, by day and by night, asking the children to imagine themselves at each setting and describe them to the group. They should use the planning grid provided in Unit 15 Resource 1: Planning the paragraph to guide them.

Embed
Ask the children to use their planning to write two atmospheric paragraphs about their chosen setting. The checklist in Unit 15 Resource 2: Conveying atmosphere supports them with this.

Challenge
Ask the children to film a setting of their choice with a camera of some kind at two different times. They should focus on creating an atmosphere through the camera shots and angles that they use or by adding a soundtrack when they edit the film. They could play it to the class and ask for feedback on how the atmosphere was conveyed.

Homework / Additional activities

Night and day
Ask the children to draw two pictures showing a place you know well at night and in the day, making them as atmospheric as possible. They should then write under each picture the type of music/soundtrack that would accompany each picture and why.

Collins Connect: Unit 15
Ask the children to complete Unit 15 (See Teach → Year 5 → Composition → Unit 15).

Unit 16: Précising longer texts

Overview

English curriculum objectives
Writing – composition
Year 5 children should be taught to:
- draft and write by précising longer passages
- evaluate and edit by assessing the effectiveness of their own and others' writing.

Building towards
Children will write a précis of a story opening.

Treasure house resources
- Composition Skills Pupil Book 5, Unit 16, pages 64–68
- Photocopiable Unit 16, Resource 1: Mowgli arrives, page 95
- Photocopiable Unit 16, Resource 2: Improving my précis, page 96

Additional resources
- Clips from the opening of either of the two Disney films of *The Jungle Book*: the original animated version (1967) or the live-action version (2016)

Introduction

Teaching overview
This unit focuses on creating a précised version of the opening of *The Jungle Book* (1894) by the English writer Rudyard Kipling as retold by Narinder Dhami. The extract tells the story of the discovery of the boy-cub Mowgli and his adoption by the wolves, Bagheera and Baloo. The extract is filled with fear and tension as the cruel tiger Shere Khan lurks in the background, threatening Mowgli. The main plot and characters of *The Jungle Book* are thus all established. To prepare for creating their précis, the children note down the key elements of the story. A précis (summary) is usually a third of the length of a text, so the children should aim to write a text of about 200 words here.

The poet, journalist and novelist Rudyard Kipling (1865–1936) became famous for his stories set in countries colonised by the British, notably India. Some consider him a controversial writer; his gifts as a storyteller, however, are undisputed.

Introduce the concept
Tell the children an anecdote about yourself, writing it down on the board as you tell it. If possible, make it quite rambling. Agree together on the key points of the anecdote and model crossing out elements and creating a new version, one third the length of the original.

Move on to discuss the children's memories of either of *The Jungle Book* films or other versions of the story they know. Remember the main plot elements and characters. Ask the children to discuss with a partner what must happen in the opening scenes to start the story off. (Possible answer: Mowgli must be brought up by wolves; the reader must meet Shere Khan; Bagheera and Baloo must take charge of Mowgli.)

Read the extract dramatically to the children, bringing out the tension and ensuring that they understand the story that is taking place beyond the cave. Compare the opening in the extract to their memory of the opening of the film. Agree that it is much longer and gives more details about how Mowgli arrives with the wolves. Explain that their task today is to create their own, equally dramatic, shorter version of the extract (*not* the film). Display an enlarged version of Unit 16 Resource 1: Mowgli arrives on the interactive whiteboard or similar and work together to cut about two-thirds of the text. Verbally create a new version, showing how some parts need to be reworded.

Unit 16: Précising longer texts

Pupil practice

Pupil Book pages 64–68

Get started

Ask the children to read the extract with a partner and discuss the answer to each question. Encourage them to share evidence for their answers in the text.

Answers

1. Mother Wolf (wolf), Father Wolf (wolf), Shere Khan (tiger), Akela (wolf), Baloo (brown bear), Bagheera (panther)
2. Shere Khan believes that the baby is part of the human party he was hunting.
3. Mother Wolf probably wants to save the baby because she has her own cubs and Mowgli inspires her maternal instincts.
4. The wolves, like the other animals, do not like Shere Khan because he does not follow the law of the jungle (he kills humans).
5. The atmosphere for most of the extract is tense: the wolves sit in a dark cave listening to a tiger hunting. The arrival of Mowgli breaks this tension but the sudden appearance of Shere Khan at the mouth of the cave would make an audience jump in the cinema. The council at the rock begins tensely as the wolves debate, Shere Khan arrives and the fate of the baby is uncertain. This eases as Mother Wolf, Bagheera and Baloo speak.
6. The law of the jungle is the code the animals live by. It includes not killing and eating humans (it would lead to other humans coming).

Try these

Children answer 'summary' questions about the extract.

Possible answers

1. The wolves hear Shere Khan hunting. Baby Mowgli is taken in by the wolves. Shere Khan the tiger says that Mowgli belongs to him. The wolves have a council meeting about the baby. Bagheera and Baloo say they will help bring up Mowgli. [5 marks]
2. Baby Mowgli is taken in by the wolves. Shere Khan the tiger says that Mowgli belongs to him. Bagheera and Baloo say that they will help to bring up Mowgli. [3 marks]

Now try these

Children write a précised version of the extract, about 200 words in length. Accept any précised passages that are about the right length and include the key characters and events.

You may wish to use photocopiables in **Support and Embed** to give differentiated support with these activities.

Support, embed & challenge

Support

Unit 16 Resource 1: Mowgli arrives provides a shorter extract to précis and should be used with children who need support with the activity in **Now try these**.

Possible answer

One day a little baby toddled into a cave of wolves.

"A man cub!" Father Wolf cried.

He picked the baby up and laid him next to his family.

Suddenly Shere Khan pushed his great, striped head and shoulders into the entrance.

"Give him to me!" he roared.

"Never!" Mother Wolf cried. "He'll live with our pack."

"We'll see," the angry tiger snapped. "As soon as I get the chance, I'll kill him!"

Embed

Ask the children to reread the original opening and then discuss with a partner what has been lost in their précis (probably drama and atmosphere). They should make some notes and then replace two sentences of their choosing back into the opening to improve the drama and atmosphere. Ask them to make a final draft, proofreading for spelling and punctuation errors. Unit 16 Resource 2: Improving my précis provides a template for this.

Challenge

Ask the children to write a one-page précis (200 words) of a book of their choice.

Homework / Additional activities

Writing prose

Watch the clip from the film or animated versions of *The Jungle Book* and make notes about the scene where Mowgli is kidnapped by the monkeys and taken to see King Louie (as a series of bullet points or as a story map). Ask the children to write a prose version of the scene.

Unit 17: Using organisational features

Overview

English curriculum objectives

Writing – composition

Year 5 children should be taught to plan their writing by noting and developing initial ideas, drawing on reading and research where necessary.

Year 5 children should be taught to draft and write by using further organisational and presentational devices to structure text and to guide the reader.

Building towards

Children will write and create an eye-catching poster about the Solar System.

Treasure house resources

- Composition Skills Pupil Book 5, Unit 17, pages 69–71
- Photocopiable Unit 17, Resource 1: Elements for my Solar System poster, page 97
- Photocopiable Unit 17, Resource 2: Solar System notes, page 98

Additional resources

- A range of books and websites about the Solar System
- A range of non-fiction texts on space in general, particularly those with an attractive design and a range of organisational features
- A computer presentation package, such as Microsoft PowerPoint®

Introduction

Teaching overview

This unit focuses on making notes and creating an attractive non-fiction text about the Solar System in the form of a poster. The text in the Pupil Book introduces the subject and the children are asked to take notes from it. These notes then need to be enhanced by further research and used to create a poster that includes headings, 'fun fact' boxes, photographs and captions.

Introduce the concept

Provide each group of children with a pile of non-fiction books about space. Give them a few minutes to find three interesting facts that they want to share with the class, making notes including the key information. Remind them that when note-taking we write key words, not full sentences, and can use arrows and lines, circles and symbols. Model finding an interesting fact in one of the books and making a note about it on the board. Share the facts. Next ask the children to return to their pile of books and find five different organisational features in them. Create a list of the features they have found, for example headings, subheadings, photos, diagrams, captions, fact boxes.

Read the extract together and discuss the meaning of any tricky words.

Pupil practice

Pupil Book pages 69–71

Get started

Ask the children to reread the text in pairs. Ask them to find the answers to the following questions.

Answers

1. The Asteroid Belt
2. Any two from: Mercury, Venus, Earth or Mars
3. Any two from: Jupiter, Saturn, Uranus or Neptune
4. The Kuiper Belt
5. Bigger

Try these

Children answer questions about features that would enhance the text.

Suggested answers

1. Accept any suitable answer, for example: The Solar System, Amazing Space, Spinning around the Sun, and so on. [1 mark]
2. Accept any suitable answers, for example: The planets, The Asteroid Belt, The Kuiper Belt, Moons, Comets. [1 mark for each; 5 in total]

Unit 17: Using organisational features

3. Accept any two reasonable questions that are linked to the text, for example: Why is Pluto no longer a planet? How did the Solar System begin? How old is the Solar System? Are there other planets? Are there any other Solar Systems? Will the Sun ever die? Is there life on any other planet? Which is the biggest planet? Has anyone ever travelled to another planet? [1 mark for each question; 2 in total]

4. Accept any caption that enhances the image, for example: Eight planets orbit the Sun. Earth is the third planet from the Sun. The planets all spin round the Sun on the same plane. [1 mark]

Now try these

1 and 2. The children copy out the chart or use Resource 2 and make notes about the extract. Remind them that they should write only key words on the chart. They do some extra research and add two fun facts.

Example Answers

Planets	Asteroid Belt
Mercury, Venus, Earth, Mars = small + rocky	between Mars and Jupiter
Jupiter, Saturn, Uranus, Neptune = large + gassy.	millions of chunks of rocks = asteroids
They all orbit the Sun.	

Moons	Kuiper Belt
Earth and gassy planets – moons	past Neptune – belt of ice chunks
Saturn, Uranus + Neptune – rings of ice particles	

Comets	Fun facts
lumps of ice and dust near Sun → tail	accept any on-topic fun fact

3. They use their notes to write and create a Solar System poster, including title, headings, subheadings, 'fun facts', illustration and caption.

You may wish to use photocopiables in **Support and Embed** to give differentiated support with these activities.

Support, embed & challenge

Support
Ask the children, working in pairs or in small groups, to cut out the elements from Unit 17 Resource 1: Elements for my Solar System poster (subheadings and texts) and to use them to create an information poster by sticking down texts and headings correctly paired. Ask the children to write a brief introduction together and to add an illustration of the Solar System, either a printout or their own. They should also decide where the 'Fun facts' and Glossary should go.

Embed
Ask the children to use Unit 17 Resource 2: Solar System notes to make notes from the extract and from further research, and then use these to create an eye-catching information poster on the Solar System. They should use as many of the features outlined in the unit as they can. Ask them to find suitable illustrations to print out or to draw their own.

Challenge
Ask the children to research space exploration and use their notes to add another section to their poster.

Homework / Additional activities

Non-fiction on a computer
Organise for children to recreate their non-fiction text on the computer. A presentation package is an easy way to add images, videos and captions.

Unit 18: Building cohesion

Overview

English curriculum objectives

Writing – composition

Year 5 children should be taught to plan their writing by noting and developing initial ideas, drawing on reading and research where necessary.

Year 5 children should be taught to draft and write by:

- selecting appropriate grammar and vocabulary, understanding how such choices can change and enhance meaning
- using a wide range of devices to build cohesion within and across paragraphs.

Building towards

Children will write an 'email from space', using adverbials and other techniques to build cohesion.

Treasure house resources

- Composition Skills Pupil Book 5, Unit 18, pages 72–73
- Photocopiable Unit 18, Resource 1: Useful linking phrases, page 99
- Photocopiable Unit 18, Resource 2: *Saturn V* rocket launch, page 100

Additional resources

- Clip of a rocket launch for one of the lunar missions or the launch scene from the film *Apollo 13* (1995), which shows the launch sequence very clearly
- A range of suitable internet sites and books about space for children to browse and read

Introduction

Teaching overview

This unit provides practice in using a range of devices – for example adverbials of time, place and number, relative clauses and pronouns – to create cohesion and flow through an explanation text. The children read a quirky tourist guide to space exploration and repurpose the information, enhancing it with their own research, to write an email detailing an astronaut's first day in space. Photocopiable pages provide lists of adverbials to use and a description of a launch to make notes from.

Introduce the concept

Display an enlarged version of Unit 18 Resource 2: *Saturn V* rocket launch and read it with the children – this will help them to understand the launching process. Play the launch scene from *Apollo 13* (choosing carefully to avoid showing anyone smoking), which clearly and dramatically shows some of these elements. Next, return to the information text and ask volunteers to find any adverbials or any other cohesive devices. Explain to the children that they will be using this text and the text in the Pupil Book as sources for writing their own email written by an astronaut after his or her first day in space.

Pupil practice

Pupil Book pages 72–73

Get started

Children discuss their thoughts and feelings about space travel with a partner. Remind the children that they should be doing as much listening as talking. Listen out for children sharing ideas and listening well. Ask them to write down two questions about space travel – provide books and internet access so that children can research the answers. Ask the children to share their findings.

Try these

Children look in the text to find the answers to the questions.

Answers

1. Because the force of gravity pulls all objects to the Earth. [1 mark]
2. Your body becomes very heavy as it is pulled backwards. [1 mark]
3. As the various fuel tanks are emptied they detached from the spacecraft; the spacecraft becomes much smaller. [1 mark]
4. Without gravity, objects float around. [1 mark]
5. Without gravity, liquids form into floating blobs. [1 mark]

Unit 18: Building cohesion

Now try these

Children pretend that they are an astronaut just launched successfully into space and write an email that both incorporates facts about space and captures the emotions of the astronaut. Look for linking phrases that create cohesive writing (rather than a list of statements).

You may wish to use the activities and photocopiables in **Support and Embed** to give differentiated support with **Now try these**.

Support, embed & challenge

Support

Ask these children to work in a group with assistance from a teacher. Set the scene: they are astronauts in space having just successfully launched earlier that day. They have spent a few hours in orbit checking their instruments, eating dinner and resting. Cut out the words and phrases from use Unit 18 Resource 1: Useful linking phrases and place them in the middle of the group. Ask the children to take turns to pick up a word or phrase and use it in a sentence about their day as an astronaut. Scribe the sentences for the children, leaving them displayed as they start to write their email home.

Embed

Ask the children to use Unit 18 Resource 2: *Saturn V* rocket launch to research and makes notes, so as to find more vivid detail for their 'email from space'. Remind the children that a successful email will have linking phrases and words to make their email easy to read; an unsuccessful email will be a series of statements. Once they have finished their first draft, ask them to read their email aloud, with emotion, to a partner. Tell them to listen out for places where their email sounds disjointed – it might be difficult to read at this point. With a partner's help, ask the children to improve the flow of their email before writing – and illustrating – a final version.

Challenge

Ask the children to take on the role of 'cohesion doctor' and help other children in the class improve their work.

Homework / Additional activities

Emails from Mars

Ask the children to find out about planned Mars missions. Ask them to write an email home from an astronaut on his or her one-way trip to Mars.

Unit 19: Funny stories

Overview

English curriculum objectives
Writing – composition

Year 5 children should be taught to draft and write by, in writing narratives, describing settings, characters and atmosphere and integrating dialogue to convey character and advance the action.

Building towards
Children will write their own funny scene, as a continuation of Toad's adventures.

Treasure house resources
- Composition Skills Pupil Book 5, Unit 19, pages 74–78
- Photocopiable Unit 19, Resource 1: Toad flying high, page 101
- Photocopiable Unit 19, Resource 2: Planning a new adventure for Toad, page 102

Additional resources
- An audiobook reading of *The Wind in the Willows*
- Age-appropriate silly scenes of the 'You've Been Framed' variety from the internet

Introduction

Teaching overview
This unit focuses on writing a new comic scene using a character and setting previously encountered. The children read an extract from *The Wind in the Willows* (1908) by the Scottish writer Kenneth Grahame (1859–1932), as retold by Nicky Singer. They discuss the comic elements in the story: the character of Toad and the muddle his own actions get him into. They practise telling their own funny story based on an experience of their own, then move on to plan, orally rehearse and write their own episode for Mr Toad.

Introducing the concept
Earlier in the week, listen to an extract from an audio reading of *The Wind in the Willows* so the children are familiar with the character of Toad and the story so far. Tell the children a silly story about yourself. Model writing it down, bringing out the humour through the language and dialogue. Talk about the ways writers make a story funny, such as creating drama, adding dialogue and so on. Read the extract from *The Wind in the Willows* in the Pupil Book.

Pupil practice
Pupil Book pages 74–78

Get started
Children reread the extract and discuss the questions with a partner before writing down their answers.

Answers
1. Toad is rude to anyone who he thinks has insulted him. He can be charming when he wants to.
   [Accept any reasonable answer; 1 mark]
2. Toad is a liar. He is a chancer and is good at taking advantage of any situation. He is arrogant and often feels sorry for himself.   [Accept any reasonable answer; 2 marks]
3. Toad is funny because he thinks so highly of himself but behaves so badly and ridiculously.
   [2 marks]
4. The situation is funny because elegant, arrogant Toad is dressed as a washerwoman. This is funny in itself but it leads to further humour as he has to actually do some washing and he's not very good at it.   [Accept any reasonable answer; 2 marks]
5. The dialogue adds humour when Toad is outrageously rude and when he lies.   [Accept any reasonable answer; 2 marks]

Try these
Children practise telling their funny story in their head before telling it to a partner. Ask brave children to tell their funny story to the class. Afterwards, discuss what made the stories funny. Compliment children on their pace and delivery and talk about the elements of each situation that make it funny.

Now try these
Children choose one of the two options in the Pupil Book and then plan and write their funny episode. Ensure that the children spend time planning (using Unit 19 Resource 2: Planning a new adventure for Toad) and rehearsing their story before finally writing it. Remind them to include dialogue – between Toad and the various people he upsets.

You may wish to use the activities and photocopiables in **Support and Embed** to give differentiated support with the writing project in **Now try these**.

Unit 19: Funny stories

Support, embed & challenge

Support
Ask the children to work in groups using Unit 19 Resource 1: Toad flying high to make up a story to go with the pictures. Have the children take turns around the group looking at a picture and continuing the plot. Discuss what might go into each speech bubble, asking the children to make their own choice for themselves. Ask the children to practise telling the whole story, recording it for them when they have polished it.

Embed
Ask the children to use Unit 19 Resource 2: Planning a new adventure for Toad to help them plan a new adventure for Toad and to work out a controlled build-up to the final catastrophe Mr Toad creates. Once the children have planned their story, encourage them to attempt to use their notes to tell an oral version to a partner. This should throw up any holes in their plot, places where the comedy can be brought out, and so on. Tell them to revisit their plans before writing out a draft story.

You could ask children to write a final version in a booklet with a front cover and back-cover blurb. Encourage them to add comic illustrations.

Challenge
Challenge these children to learn their comic episode by heart and deliver it to the rest of the class as a told story, complete with all the drama that entails. Remind them that, if they are lucky enough to make everyone laugh, they should pause for the laughter to finish before they continue.

Homework / Additional activities

Future comedians
Ask the children to ask members of their family to tell them funny anecdotes about when they were young. Ask them to practise and then share these stories back in school.

Ask the children to each learn two new (excellent and appropriate for school) jokes. Tell them to practise telling their jokes with the right intonation and drama (and punch line). Award particular praise for those who have researched and delivered particularly fine and/or unknown jokes.

Unit 20: List poems

Overview

English curriculum objectives

Writing – composition

Year 5 children should be taught to plan their writing by identifying the audience for and purpose of the writing, selecting the appropriate form and using other similar writing as models for their own.

Year 5 children should be taught to draft and write by selecting appropriate grammar and vocabulary, understanding how such choices can change and enhance meaning.

Building towards

Children will write their own list poem.

Treasure house resources

- Composition Skills Pupil Book 5, Unit 20, pages 79–81
- Photocopiable Unit 20, Resource 1: Snowy day, page 103
- Photocopiable Unit 20, Resource 2: Scary vocabulary, page 104

Additional resources

- Positive images of winter scenes: people having fun, beautiful scenery, and so on

Introduction

Teaching overview

A list poem is a straightforward form of poetry in which the poet builds up details by listing items about the subject. Most children of this age will be able to write a pleasing list poem by gathering up items around the subject and listing them. The two poems provided as templates in this unit are slightly more complex than a straight list. The first, 'Don't Look Round!', is a list of sentences and phrases often starting with the repeated phrase 'I'm the …'. It lists all the irrational fears we might have as we lie in bed at night or if we are walking somewhere. 'Winter Days' builds up a picture of freezing days that bite and make us want to stay in bed.

The children are set the task of choosing to write their own poetic answer to one of the poems: either a poem listing all the things they are not scared of; or writing a positive poem about snowy weather that makes the poet want to leap out of bed and run outside. Because the format of these poems is straightforward, the children should be encouraged to ensure they have chosen the best words – working on interesting noun phrases where appropriate.

Introducing the concept

Read 'Don't Look Round!' to the children, sounding dramatic and menacing. Give the children a minute to discuss the main idea of the poem with a partner before asking them to share their thoughts. Agree that it is about the things that frighten us that are in our imagination. Talk about the way we can sometimes let these fears take hold of us – particularly as we listen to the house creak at night. Point out the poem's structure: the build-up of items, the repeated phrase, the change in pace, the 'jump' end.

Move on to 'Winter Days' – a poem about a completely different way of being miserable. Ask the children to immerse themselves in the chill of the poem as you read it aloud. Then discuss the different details that create this effect.

Pupil practice

Pupil Book pages 79–81

Get started

Ask the children to read the poems again with a partner, reading and discussing the meaning of the annotations at the side. Ask them to answer the comprehension questions.

Suggested answers

1. It is about the sounds we hear at night and our irrational fear of them, and the feeling of having someone unknown behind you – when there isn't anyone there. [2 marks]
2. 'Behind You' is the imaginary scary person, monster or thing that we become scared of when we can't think of another explanation. [2 marks]
3. The house creaking at night as the temperature changes, rain on branches on the window, the wind. [2 marks]
4. 'Biting wind', 'Winds blow', 'Snow', 'Ice in lanes', 'Frosty patterns'. [5 marks]

Unit 20: List poems

5. Five of 'Noses red', 'Lips sore', 'Runny eyes', 'Hands raw', 'Cars crawl', 'Slush in gutters'. [5 marks]

6. Because when they lift their head out of bed, they can feel how cold the day is and they want to stay in the warmth of their bed. [1 mark]

Try these

1. Children return to 'Don't Look Round!' and discuss how it makes them feel. They talk about the sounds they can hear as they lie in bed at night and the things they are or used to be frightened of. Ask them to share feelings sensitively. Listen carefully to the conversations, supporting children who become upset. Remind the children to listen carefully to each other. They write down their ideas as a list of noun phrases.

2. Ask the children to draw up a list of positive things about snowy days. Use the children's ideas to create a long class list.

Now try these

Ask the children to choose one of the poems to write. Read through and discuss the different ideas listed before the children start, and encourage them to try out ideas out loud or in note form before writing. If they are writing the scary poem, ask the children to write a list of statements starting 'I'm not frightened of...' and ending each with another frightening element. They should finish the poem with a slightly different line, for example: 'I'm not scared of anything (except broccoli)'.

Accept all attempts at poems that build a picture through building up lists of different fears or snowy elements.

You may wish to use the activities and photocopiables in **Support and Embed** to give differentiated support with the writing tasks in **Now try these**.

Support, embed & challenge

Support

Focus with these children on writing a poem about a snowy day. Using Unit 20 Resource 1: Snowy day, children create some interesting noun phrases that they can draw on when they come to write their poem. They can then cut out their noun phrases and spend time arranging them into stanzas. Let the children stick their phrases down then spend time editing their first draft.

Embed

Once the children have finished the first draft of their chosen poem, provide them with a copy of either Unit 20 Resource 1: Snowy day or Unit 20 Resource 2: Scary vocabulary (depending on their choice). Encourage them to cut out the vocabulary and play around with it making different phrases. Tell them to look back at their first draft and see if they can improve it by adding any of the words or phrases from the resource sheet.

Tell them to work on a second draft of their poem. Challenge them to capture exuberance in the snow poem or defiance in the poem about not being frightened. Can they play around with the speed of any lines? Finally, tell them to read their second draft out loud to check for sense, flow and errors before writing a final draft.

Challenge

Ask the children to write a companion poem to 'Winter Days' called 'Summer Days'. Challenge them to capture the feel of a hot summer day, using repetition or lists to build up different details.

Homework / Additional activities

Poetry by heart

Ask the children to learn their chosen poem by heart and perform it with confidence and a clear voice to the class. You could also ask the children to create a dramatic performance of either 'Winter Days' or 'Don't Look Round!'

Review unit 3

Pupil Book pages 82–83

These tasks provide the children with the opportunity to apply and demonstrate the skills they have learned.

Explain to the children that they now have an opportunity to show their skills independently. Read through the task with the children and make sure they have understood what to do.

A. Creating atmosphere

Look for evidence of children's developing understanding of how to create atmosphere in their narrative writing. Significant features to look out for include:

- expanded noun phrases
- strong verbs
- figurative language such as personification, metaphor or simile.

B. Organising information in non-fiction

Look for evidence of children's developing understanding of how to organise information for a non-fiction report. Significant features to look out for include:

- a heading and title
- subheadings
- diagrams or illustrations
- technical vocabulary
- summary statement.

C. Writing a humorous story

Look for evidence of children's developing understanding of the features of narrative – specifically humorous stories. Significant features to look out for include:

- a storyline where characters are found in surprising situations or a series of unfortunate – but not life-threatening – events
- characters who act in funny ways or a mismatch between a character and his or her expectations
- narrative conventions, such as past tense, third person, subject/verb agreement.

Unit 1 Resource 1

Planning my persuasive argument

Opening and main point of my argument	
Paragraph 1	Supporting point 1
Paragraph 2	Supporting point 2
Paragraph 3	Supporting point 3
Conclusion	

Unit 1 Resource 2

My persuasive argument

Write your complete article, using your plan to remind you what to include. Use the checklist to help you.

Write your argument here.

___

Checklist

- Introduce your point.

- Organise your arguments into paragraphs.

- Add supporting arguments.

- Include adverbials to link your points.

- Add a conclusion.

Unit 2 Resource 1

Planning the next episode

The Billeting Officer and the evacuees go to the village hall and wait for the other villagers to come and choose a child.
Plan what happens next by adding drawings with speech bubbles to the storyboard and making notes underneath each one.

1	2

3	4

Unit 2 Resource 2

Writing the next episode

The Billeting Officer and the evacuees go to the village hall and wait for the other villagers to come and choose a child.

Use your plan to help you write the next episode below.

_____
_____
_____
_____
_____
_____
_____
_____
_____
_____
_____
_____
_____
_____
_____
_____

Checklist

- Write in the past tense.
- Use dialogue to move the action on.
- Describe the setting.
- Make the episode realistic.

Unit 3 Resource 1

My simile poem

Write your own poem about clouds using similes.

Write three things that clouds remind you of.

1. _____

2. _____

3. _____

Use your ideas to write the poem.

The clouds are like _____

(Now write what they are doing)

_____

_____

The clouds are like _____

(Now write what they are doing)

_____

_____

The clouds are like _____

(Now write what they are doing)

_____

_____

Unit 3 Resource 2

My metaphor poem

Choose the title of your poem:

- Snow
- Clouds
- Friends

Write three things that your topic reminds you of.

1. _____

2. _____

3. _____

Use your ideas to write a poem with three metaphors. Follow the example given.

Example: *Clouds are white cotton wool balls floating in the sky.*

1. _____

2. _____

3. _____

Unit 4 Resource 1

Stage directions

Add some simple stage directions in the brackets.

Remember:

- Show how the character should act as they speak their lines.
- Tell the actors when their character should enter and exit.

Cinderella: (_____) I wish I could go to the ball.
Ugly Sister: (_____) Ha! You? Look at your clothes and your hair. You are so ugly the prince would never want to dance with you.
Cinderella: (_____) But I promise I'll work even harder if you let me go!
Ugly Sister: (_____) Go and clean the floor. I must go and get myself ready for the ball. (_____)
Cinderella: (_____) Oh dear, what shall I do? I've got to clean the floor. (_____)
Fairy Godmother: (_____) But you shall go to the ball! (_____) Watch my wand!
Cinderella: (_____) My dress! It's so beautiful.

Unit 4 Resource 2

The glass slipper

Write a playscript version of this scene from 'Cinderella'.

Remember use this format:
[Character's name]: [stage directions][What they say]

Example
Annabel: (looking around) I think I'm lost!

Scene 1:

_____ : (_____) _____

_____ : (_____) _____

_____ : (_____) _____

_____ : (_____) _____

_____ : (_____) _____

_____ : (_____) _____

_____ : (_____) _____

_____ : (_____) _____

_____ : (_____) _____

_____ : (_____) _____

_____ : (_____) _____

_____ : (_____) _____

_____ : (_____) _____

_____ : (_____) _____

_____ : (_____) _____

_____ : (_____) _____

Unit 5 Resource 1

Letter to a friend

Write your letter below, remembering to set it out as you have been shown. Use the checklist as a prompt.

Write your letter here.

Checklist

- Address your reader directly.
- Use the first person.
- Use the past tense.
- Organise your information into paragraphs.
- Add your thoughts and feelings.

Unit 5 Resource 2

Magazine article

Write your school magazine article below. Use the checklist as a prompt.

Write your article here.

_____

Checklist

- Describe the events chronologically.
- Organise your information into paragraphs.
- Use the third person.
- Use the past tense.
- Use formal language.

Unit 6 Resource 1

Police report

Complete the police report below as you report the finding of the strange egg in the school playground.

Reporting officer: _Inspector Strangeways_

Date of incident: _____

Time of incident: _____

Location of incident: _____

Statement: (Use first person and describe the events in the order in which they happened. Include the relevant facts and details only.)

_____
_____
_____
_____
_____
_____
_____

Diagram to show where the incident happened:

Unit 6 Resource 2

Diary entry

Write your diary entry here.
Describe what happened and include what you thought and felt.

Dear Diary,

Something amazing happened at school today...

Checklist

Have I included...

- thoughts and feelings?
- hopes and wishes?
- is my language informal and personal?
- date of events?
- description of events?

Unit 7 Resource 1

Planning my narrative poem

Setting _____

_____

Characters _____

_____

Summary of storyline _____

_____

_____

_____

_____

_____

Beginning	Middle	End

Moral of the story _____

_____

Rhyme scheme I will use _____

_____

Unit 7 Resource 2

Writing my narrative poem

Use the planning grid for your narrative poem to now write your poem in full.

Add an illustration to your poem here.

Unit 8 Resource 1

Adding linking words and phrases

Choose a connecting word or phrase from the options given to complete the sentences.

1. There are some countries where the rains fail _____ _____ (and / in addition) there is drought.

2. _____ (furthermore / consequently) the crops wither.

3. _____ (for this reason / if) the population may go without food.

4. _____ (if / unless) this continues, people begin to starve.

5. _____ (furthermore / by contrast) the seed that should be saved for planting next year's crop needs to be used right away.

Unit 8 Resource 2

My sentences

Use connecting words and phrases from the box, or ideas of your own, to write sentences.

also	in addition	furthermore	consequently	therefore
as a result	nonetheless	on the other hand	but
for example	similarly	moreover	in conclusion

1. _____

2. _____

3. _____

4. _____

5. _____

6. _____

7. _____

8. _____

9. _____

10. _____

Unit 9 Resource 1

Goldilocks and Baby Bear

Plan your version of 'Goldilocks and the three bears' from the perspective of Goldilocks. Remember to use the first person when you write the story.

Make notes for your story:

- Why does Goldilocks go into the house?

- Does she feel guilty for eating the porridge and breaking the chair?

- Does she know that bears live in the house?

My character: _____

Now plan Baby Bear's story here. Remember to use the first person when you write.

_____
_____
_____
_____
_____
_____
_____
_____

Unit 9 Resource 2

A trip to the zoo

Plan two matching short stories about a trip to the zoo: one from the perspective of a child; one from the perspective of an animal.

Child's perspective: my character:
• Who does the child go with?
• How does he/she feel about the animals?
• What is his/her favourite animal?
• Do they watch any 'feeding times'?
• What happens at the end?

_____
_____
_____
_____
_____
_____
_____
_____

Unit 10 Resource 1

Plan for a conversation in a shop

Write a plan for a conversation that might happen in a shop. Describe the characters involved.

Your plan for the conversation (What is it about? Who, roughly, will say what?):

A short description of the characters:

Unit 10 Resource 2

Dialogue in a shop

Write the dialogue for the conversation in the shop.
Remember to follow the rules for setting out speech in stories!

_____
_____
_____
_____
_____
_____
_____
_____
_____
_____
_____
_____
_____
_____
_____

Checklist for the use of dialogue:

- show what people think and feel

- show relationships

- move the plot forward

- impart information to the reader.

Unit 11 Resource 1

Planning my persuasive letter

Plan your letter by making notes to answer the questions.

Address and date Where will you put this?	
Formal greeting Do you know the name of the person you are writing to?	
First paragraph Introduce your complaint and the change you would like to see.	
Second and third paragraphs Make your points, providing the facts or evidence you need to support your argument.	
Connecting words or phrases Linking your paragraphs	
Sign-off If you know the person's name, use 'Yours sincerely'; if you don't, use 'Yours faithfully'.	

Unit 11 Resource 2

My persuasive letter

Write your persuasive letter here. Use the notes you made previously. Write in full sentences and use formal language.

_____
_____
_____
_____
_____
_____
_____
_____
_____
_____
_____
_____
_____
_____

Letter conventions checklist

- sender's address at top right-hand corner

- date beneath the sender's address

- recipient's address on the left-hand side, after the line with the date on

- greeting – do you know the person's name?

- use of paragraphs to structure what you want to say

- sign-off – check that you have used the right form.

Unit 12 Resource 1

My newspaper report

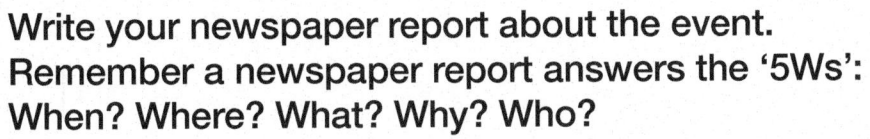

Write your newspaper report about the event.
Remember a newspaper report answers the '5Ws':
When? Where? What? Why? Who?

Unit 12 Resource 2

My newspaper editorial

Write your editorial here. Give the facts of what happened, but, more importantly, explain your opinions and how you feel about the issue. Begin with a headline.

Unit 13 Resource 1

A tale for older children

Retell your chosen traditional tale using the language and other features similar to those used in the first extract.
Use the checklist to help you.

_____
_____
_____
_____
_____
_____
_____
_____
_____
_____
_____
_____
_____
_____

Checklist

Have I used ...

- a variety of verbs?
- long paragraphs?
- different verbs to replace 'said'?
- complex sentences?
- dialogue (direct speech)?
- adverbs of manner?

Unit 13 Resource 2

A tale for younger children

Adapt your chosen traditional tale for younger readers.

Use the checklist to help you.

___

Checklist
Have I used ...
• simple vocabulary?
• single sentences (rather than paragraphs)?
• simple sentences and words?
• indirect speech – for example, 'The woman said that' – rather than dialogue?
• illustrations?

Unit 14 Resource 1

Planning the description

Complete the table by adding words and phrases to describe your chosen setting.

Sights	Sounds	Smells

Alliterative phrases _____

Simile _____

Metaphor _____

Personification _____

Exaggeration for effect (hyperbole) _____

Unit 14 Resource 2

My descriptive paragraph

Write your descriptive paragraph here. Use your planning and the checklist provided.

_____
_____
_____
_____
_____
_____
_____
_____
_____
_____
_____
_____
_____
_____
_____

Checklist

Have I used ...

- varied vocabulary?
- noun phrases?
- interesting verbs?
- adverbs?

- simile and metaphor?
- personification?
- alliteration?
- hyperbole?

Unit 15 Resource 1

Planning the paragraph

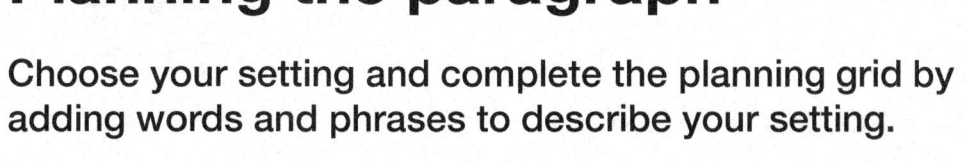

Choose your setting and complete the planning grid by adding words and phrases to describe your setting.

	My setting by day	**My setting at night**
Sights		
Sounds		
Smells		
Adjectives		
Verbs		
Adverbs		
Emotions		

Unit 15 Resource 2

Conveying atmosphere

Write two paragraphs here.
Use the ideas from your planning grid (Resource 1).

Paragraph 1 – day

Paragraph 2 – night

Unit 16 Resource 1

Mowgli arrives

Read this retelling of the opening of **'The Jungle Book'** by **Rudyard Kipling**.

Create a shorter version of the passage by crossing out the words that you don't need. Then, write a short version using the words that are left. Remember: you will need to change some of the words to make your version make sense.

Make your précis about 50–75 words long.

"It's time to go hunting," said Father Wolf. Inside the cave the four squealing cubs were playing close to their mother.
"Wait!" Mother Wolf said, pricking up her ears. "Something's coming towards our cave!"
The great wolf crouched on his back legs, ready to spring. But to his amazement, he saw a little baby who was just old enough to walk. The baby looked up into the wolf's face and laughed.
"A man cub!" Father Wolf cried. "Left behind by the humans!"
"Bring him to me," Mother Wolf called.
Gently, Father Wolf picked the baby up in his jaws. He carried him into the cave and laid him next to his family.
"How little he is!" said Mother Wolf.
Suddenly the cave grew dark. Shere Khan had pushed his great, striped head and shoulders into the entrance, blocking out the moonlight.
"The man cub is mine!" he snarled, his roar filling the cave with thunder. "Give him to me!"
Mother Wolf sprang to her feet. "Never!" she cried. "He'll live with our pack."
"We'll see," the angry tiger snapped. "The man cub belongs to me. And as soon as I get the chance, I'll kill him!"

Your précis

_____
_____
_____
_____
_____

Unit 16 Resource 2

Improving my précis

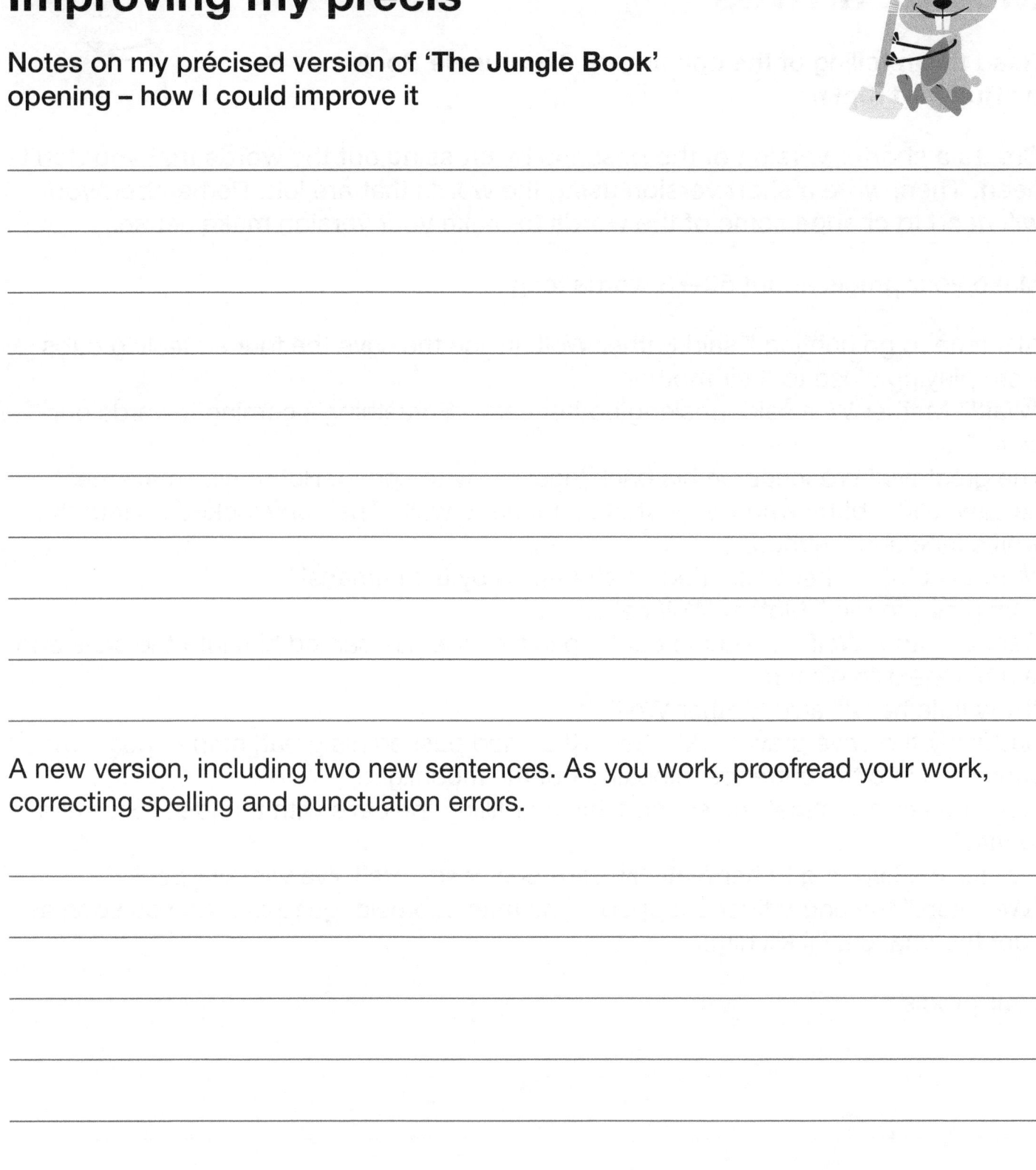

Notes on my précised version of 'The Jungle Book' opening – how I could improve it

_____
_____
_____
_____
_____
_____
_____
_____
_____
_____
_____
_____

A new version, including two new sentences. As you work, proofread your work, correcting spelling and punctuation errors.

_____
_____
_____
_____
_____
_____
_____
_____

Unit 17 Resource 1

Elements for my Solar System poster

Cut out these elements and use them to create a poster about the Solar System.

Write a short introduction for your poster and use the subheadings provided below.

Find an image of the Solar System to copy or cut out and add to your poster.

Subheadings

Planets	**Moons**	**Comets**	**Useful words**
Asteroid Belt	**Kuiper Belt**	**Fun facts**	

The Earth is one of eight planets orbiting the Sun. Mercury is nearest the Sun, followed by Venus, Earth, Mars, Jupiter, Saturn, Uranus and Neptune.

The Sun is our closest star.

It took the Voyager 1 probe 36 years to travel from Earth to the edge of the Solar System.

Some planets have moons orbiting around them. The big gas planets have many moons – for instance, Jupiter has 63.

The Earth is the third planet from the Sun.

Saturn, Uranus and Neptune also have rings. These are collections of small ice particles that form a ring around the planet.

Between Mars and Jupiter there is an area where millions of chunks of rock orbit the Sun. The rock pieces are asteroids and the area is the Asteroid Belt.

Comets are small lumps of ice covered by a frozen crust of dust. When comets travel close to the Sun, some of the ice and dust boils off into space, making a long 'tail'.

asteroid – a rock that travels through space

orbit – to continually go round another object

probe – a small unmanned spacecraft that travels through space taking photographs and recording information

Unit 17 Resource 2

Solar System notes

Use this chart to make notes from the text.

Research the Solar System in books or on the internet.
Add further information and two fun facts.

Use your notes to write an information text about the Solar System.
Make sure you use headings, subheadings, pictures, captions and boxes.

Planets	Asteroid Belt
Moons	**Kuiper Belt**
Comets	**Fun facts**
Caption	**Glossary**

Unit 18 Resource 1

Useful linking phrases

Cut out these linking phrases. Make up a sentence using each one.

Try to add four of these phrases to your email.

then	after that	this
firstly	secondly	at last
finally	later	meanwhile
nearby	before	once
when	suddenly	once again
waiting nervously	with a mighty explosion	now

Unit 18 Resource 2

Saturn V rocket launch

Read this explanation for how the *Saturn V* rocket transported the lunar spacecraft into orbit. Make notes (important words and phrases) in the column and use these notes to give realistic detail to your email.

	Notes
The spacecraft that took astronauts to the moon was called the *Saturn V* (five). When the rocket was ready to launch, all the systems were checked and the 'Go for launch' signal was given. First, the rocket engines at the bottom of the rocket were ignited and the rocket lifted off the ground like an enormous firework up to a height of 42 kilometres. At this point, the first section was detached from the rocket and fell away. An escape pod at the top of the rocket (in case the launch failed) was also jettisoned at this point as it had no further use. The next section of fuel was ignited and the rocket continued its climb. When this fuel had been used, the second stage was detached and fell away and the third stage engine was ignited. When the lunar spacecraft had reached orbit around the Earth (at 191 kilometres above the Earth), the engines were shut down. When the spacecraft was in the correct part of its orbit, the third engines were started again and the lunar spacecraft left orbit to go to the Moon.	

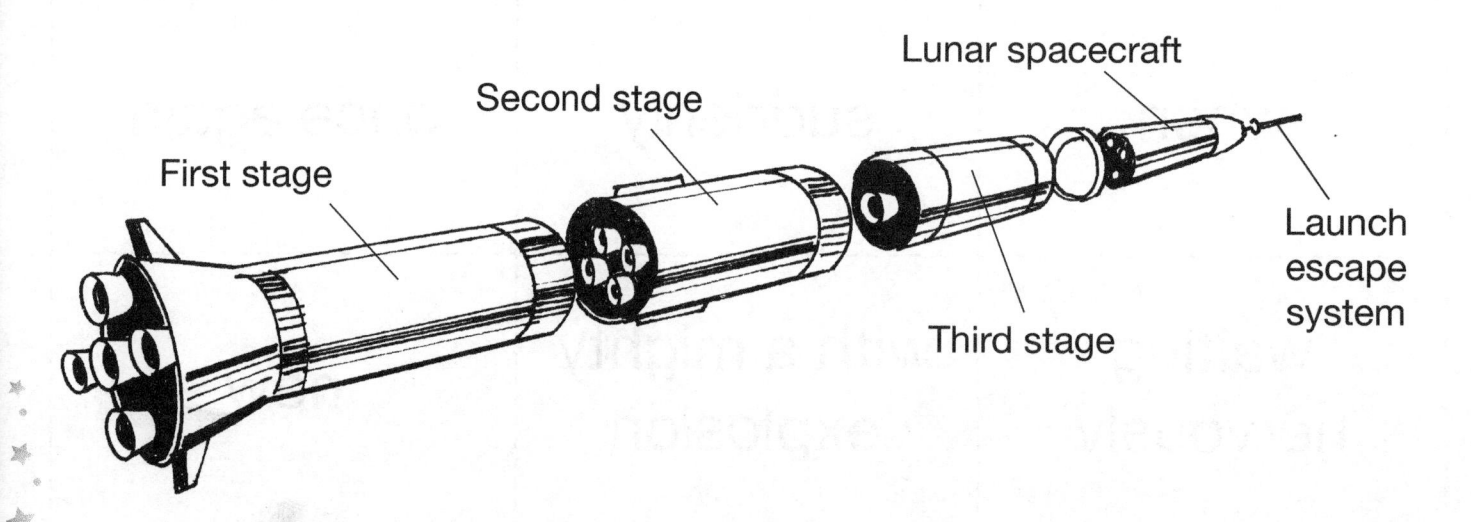

First stage — Second stage — Lunar spacecraft — Third stage — Launch escape system

Unit 19 Resource 1

Toad flying high

Use these pictures to make up a story about Toad.

Fill in the speech bubbles.

Tell your story to a partner. Then, when you are happy with it, write it down.

Unit 19 Resource 2

Planning a new adventure for Toad

Use these boxes to plan out a new adventure for Mr Toad.

Beginning	
1. Opening. The scene is set (for example, Toad starts his adventure; buys his new vehicle).	2. Things seem to be going well for Toad ...

Middle	
3. Toad begins to be thoughtless ...	4. Things go badly wrong ...

End	
5. The final disaster ...	6. Ending (for example, Toad is arrested/told off/made to feel bad/ says he's sorry)

Useful vocabulary:
One day,
At first,
But soon Toad,
Unfortunately,
All at once,

Ideas
Toad buys a plane
Toad buys a speed boat
Toad becomes a film star
Toad visits the King

Unit 20 Resource 1

Snowy day

Write a noun phrase under each of these pictures.

Cut out the noun phrases and reorder them to create the first draft of your poem.

Useful vocabulary

glistening, sliding, swooshing, lobbing, zooming, crashing, frosty, powdering, snow crystal, Grandpa's hat, piping hot, carving, cosy, fluffy

Unit 20 Resource 2

Scary vocabulary

Use this vocabulary to create phrases about not being scared. Cut out the words and use them to create different phrases, trying out different options. Add the phrases to the first draft of your poem.

I'm not scared	I'm not frightened
I don't shiver	I don't get goose-bumps
It doesn't frighten me	of
when	about
creaking	howling
crying	fighting
spiders	dark
under the bed	the cupboard under the stairs
being alone	the shadow on the wall
the wind in the trees	spelling tests